Windows &
Skylights

WILLIAM P. SPENCE

Sterling Publishing Co., Inc.
New York

DISCLAIMER

The author has made every attempt to present safe and sound building practices, but he makes no claim that the information in this book is complete or complies with every local building code.

The publisher does not warrant or guarantee any of the products described herein or perform any independent analysis in connection with any of the product information contained herein. The publisher does not assume, and expressly disclaims, any obligation to obtain and include information other than that provided by the manufacturer.

The reader is expressly warned to consider and adopt safety precautions that might be indicated by the activities herein and to avoid all potential hazards. By following the instructions contained herein, the reader willingly assumes all risks in connection with such instructions.

The author and publisher make no representation or warranties of any kind, including but not limited to the warranties of fitness for a particular purpose or merchantability, nor are any such representations implied with respect to the material set forth herein, and the publisher takes no responsibility with respect to such material. The publisher shall not be liable for any special, consequential, or exemplary damage resulting, in whole or part, from the reader's use of, or reliance upon, this material.

Library of Congress Cataloging-in-Publication Data

Spence, William Perkins, 1925–
    Windows & skylights / William P. Spence.
        p. cm. — (Building basics)
    Includes index.
    ISBN 0-8069-8107-5
    1. Windows—Design and construction. 2. Skylights—Design and construction. I. Title.
TH2275 .S65 2001
690'.8—dc21

                                                                    2001020774

Designed by Judy Morgan
Edited by Rodman P. Neumann

1 3 5 7 9 10 8 6 4 2

Published by Sterling Publishing Company, Inc.
387 Park Avenue South, New York, N.Y. 10016
© 2001 by William P. Spence
Distributed in Canada by Sterling Publishing
c/o Canadian Manda Group, One Atlantic Avenue, Suite 105
Toronto, Ontario, Canada M6K 3E7
Distributed in Great Britain and Europe by Cassell PLC
Wellington House, 125 Strand, London WC2R 0BB, England
Distributed in Australia by Capricorn Link (Australia) Pty. Ltd.
P.O. Box 704, Windsor, NSW 2756 Australia
Printed in China

Sterling ISBN 0-8069-8107-5

Contents

Selecting Windows

Windows serve many purposes and they deserve considerable attention when one is designing a new house or planning a remodeling project. They are a major architectural feature of both the exterior of the house (**1-1**) and the character of interior styling (**1-2**). They provide light and ventilation to the interior rooms and tend to bring a bit of the outdoors into the room (**1-3**). They can be used to bring solar heat into the house in the winter, yet have considerable insulating values to help maintain interior room temperatures.

Select windows based on the climatic conditions they will face. In northern climates of the northern hemisphere the retention of heat in the house is important. In southern climates of the northern hemisphere the blocking of solar heat from the interior is important.

Courtesy Weather Shield Windows & Doors

1-1 Windows complement the architectural mass of the house and are the major architectural feature.

1-2 Windows can provide a dramatic interior architectural feature.

ENERGY EFFICIENCY

It is very important to select windows with high energy-efficiency ratings. For many years windows were a source of major heat loss in the winter and heat gain in the summer, thus increasing heating and cooling costs. Windows now available are very energy efficient; this is a major factor to consider as selection decisions are made. Typically, double-glazed windows with a gas between the two panes of glass are almost exclusively used. Single-glazed windows with a storm window are found on older houses but are so inefficient that they are seldom used today and should be replaced with energy-efficient replacement windows when they deteriorate.

As windows are considered, look for those having the following improvements. Examine the **frame** and **sash** to see whether they are made with new materials and designed to reduce energy loss. Check to see that they have quality **weather stripping**. This reduces air infiltration, which is a major energy loser. Be certain the window has **double-glazing** with **edge spacers** that have insulation qualities, thus reducing energy loss around the edges of the glazed unit. The space between the two panes of glass should be filled with a **gas** having low thermal-conduction properties. Two gases frequently used are argon and krypton. A dead-air space without gas does have insulating properties. However, the addition of a gas improves the efficiency of the window. There are **transparent coatings** that can be placed on the glass that have a high reflection effect on long-wavelength infrared radiation. These are referred to as **low-E** coatings. They reduce the transfer of heat between the two layers of glazing. See Chapter 4 for additional information.

Following are factors to be considered as windows are selected.

1-3 Windows can connect the interior with the outdoors.

1-4 This house of traditional styling must have divided glazed lights to accurately represent the original design.

APPEARANCE

Probably the overall appearance of a window—as seen on the exterior of the house as well as how it looks from the interior—is what we pay attention to most. It is important to realize that the style of the house itself will often determine the style of window chosen. Some traditional styles should have double-hung windows with heavy muntins and small panes of glass (**1-4**). This reflects the windows used years ago when the style developed and it was difficult to produce large, flat, distortion-free panes of glass. A contemporary-style house will require totally different windows, possibly using casements and large fixed glazing units (**1-5**).

The materials used for the **window frame** and **sash** directly influence appearance. Typical choices include aluminum, composite, vinyl, solid wood, and wood clad with vinyl. The **color** is an important choice. Wood windows can be painted to match the trim on the house. The color of the others is chosen from those made available by various manufacturers. The color is directly related to the color of the siding and exterior trim, so all of these decisions must be coordinated.

1-5 This contemporary-style house utilizes large, fixed, glazed areas and casement windows.

The **size** and **shape** are related to the wall in which the window is located. The window must be in proportion to the wall area and the gable end, if one exists (**1-6**). A number of window shapes are available including triangular, circular, half-round, octagon, oval, square, and rectangular (**1-7**). Window types are discussed in detail in Chapter 3.

Consider the finish on the interior side of the window. A wood window can be stained or painted as desired. Vinyl-clad, aluminum, and vinyl windows present a limited choice for finishing the exposed interior, so interior decoration ideas must be considered as a window is selected. Some of these windows are designed so the sash is covered with wood interior trim that can be painted to match the interior woodwork (**1-8**).

Finally consider the **glazing.** Quality clear glazing is typically used and has very little distortion. Tempered glass may have a little distortion at the edges, but this is usually minimal.

The choice of glazing becomes a signifcant factor when tinted glass is used. It becomes part of the overall exterior appearance and influences how things look when you view them from the inside. Typical tints include green, blue-green, bronze, and gray. Some low-E coatings may give a slight indication of color. Tinted glazing can influence the color of interior trim, curtains, and shades or blinds. Glazing is discussed in Chapters 4 and 5.

COST CONSIDERATIONS

As decisions are made concerning the style, size, and color of window, one thought is always present—how much does the window cost? While the initial cost deserves consideration, other factors, such as appearance and energy efficiency, are of major importance. Installing a cheap, inefficient window will cost more over the years than installing a quality unit in the first place. Chances are the quality unit will operate smoothly and require little maintenance over many years.

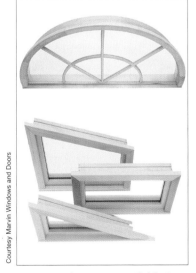

Courtesy Weather Shield Windows & Doors

Courtesy Marvin Windows and Doors

1-6 These windows are are shaped and sized in proportion to the size and mass of the exterior wall in which they are located.

1-7 Windows are available in a wide range of shapes and sizes.

Courtesy Weather Shield Windows & Doors

1-8 The interior finish on these windows matches the casing and other interior trim in the room.

Consider the cost of installing the window. In a new house this is not a major consideration, because the rough opening is framed and the window can quickly be set in place. If an old window is to be replaced, the cost of removing the old window, sizing the opening for the replacement window, installing the new window, and repairing the siding surrounding the replacement window increases the labor cost. Then consider the cost for replacing interior trim and possible repair of the gypsum wallboard or paneling. Contractors doing replacement-window work can give a price for the new window plus installation charges. Again get a quality window, and secure prices from a number of manufacturers and carpenters.

Quality windows will have better construction and materials and outlast low-quality, less expensive units. The cost per year of use for quality windows will most likely be less than those that have to be replaced sooner.

Energy-efficient windows may make the house easier to sell. This is an important feature. It is difficult to know what this may be worth in dollars, but it is usually a good investment. Likewise low-quality, deteriorated, or single-glazed windows will reduce the value of the house and make it more difficult to sell. Most buyers like to have everything shipshape.

Quality energy-efficient windows will reduce the heating and cooling costs. The amount saved will vary depending upon the climate and energy costs, but the savings are there. Energy efficiency factors are discussed in more detail in Chapter 4.

Wood windows have a higher maintenance cost than aluminum, vinyl, or vinyl-clad wood units. While having to repaint wood windows is a long-term cost, it is nonetheless something to consider. New exterior paints have enhanced properties and last a lot longer than in the past, so this maintenance chore is delayed more years than has typically been the case.

TECHNICAL CONSIDERATIONS

As window selections are made, there are a number of technical factors that should be considered. Principal among these are basic thermal and optical properties, air infiltration, energy performance, condensation resistance, and heating and cooling loads. Technical information on these factors is available on windows from various manufacturers. Organizations such as the National Fenestration Rating Council issue ratings that appear on windows. Look for the NFRC label on the window. The American Architectural Manufacturers Association has a certification program. Look for the AAMA label on the window. Information on rating systems is in Chapter 4.

RATING WINDOW PROPERTIES

For years window manufacturers issued ratings for their products. However, the parts rated and the types of test or rating procedure varied from company to company. This made it difficult for the consumer to make comparisons between the products of the many window manufacturers. Some only rated the glass but did not rate the frame. What was needed was a system to give energy ratings based on the performance of the total assembled window.

The National Fenestration Rating Council was established in 1989 to develop consistent and accurate ratings for fenestration products. Fenestration products include windows, skylights, roof windows, doors, glazed wall systems, and greenhouse and sunroom glazing.

As you select windows, the following technical properties should be considered. These are discussed in detail in the remaining chapters of this book.

U-factor is the amount of energy, in British Thermal Units, Btus, that will transfer by conduction through a window.

Visual light transmittance (VLT) is a measure of how much visible light will pass through a window.

Solar-heat-gain coefficient (SHGC) is a measure of the amount of solar heat that will pass through a window.

UV-protection is a measure of the amount of ultraviolet light blocked by coatings on glass products.

Edge spacers are materials spaced around the inside perimeter of a window.

Frame comprises the structural members forming the window and sash, which are typically wood, aluminum, vinyl, wood-resin composites, fiberglass, or PVC foam.

Air leakage, also referred to as infiltration, is the amount of air penetrating the components that make up a window.

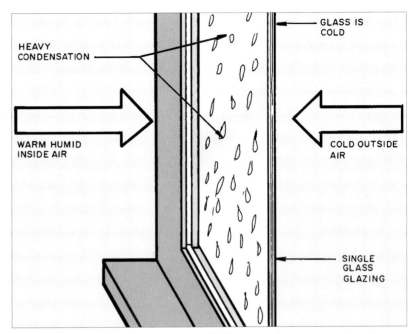

1-9 Single-glazed windows will usually have condensation in the winter when the warm, humid inside air hits the cold glass.

CONDENSATION

Condensation is a frequently occurring problem on windows. Condensation is produced when water vapor in the air comes in contact with a cold surface, such as a glass window. The vapor becomes liquid and appears on the cold surface. If the inside glass is warmer than the outside air, less condensation will occur. Double- and triple-glazed windows are less likely to have condensation than single-glazed units, because the inside glass is warmer. However, condensation is caused by moisture in the air, not by the type of window; so, if the air in the house has high humidity, even energy-efficient windows can have condensation on them. Likewise, condensation can occur on the walls and ceilings if high humidity is present. This can be very damaging to the wall finish and, if the wall does not have a vapor barrier, the mois-ture will penetrate into the wall cavity, damaging the studs and insulation. Controlling the humidity in the air is important to controlling condensation on windows, walls, and ceilings.

Some manufacturers make condensation-resistance tests to determine the **Condensation Resistance Factor (CRF)**. Such tests can be made in accordance with the American Architectural Manufacturers Association Standard *AAMA 1503.1*.

The National Fenestration Rating Council also has a condensation-resistance rating. The higher the CRF rating of a window, the less likely the window will have condensation form on it. It is recommended that windows have a CRF rating above 35.

Single-glazed windows are especially prone to condensation because they rapidly become cold in the winter and, when moisture-laden warm interior air hits them, condensation is formed (1-9). If there is enough moisture in the air in the house, the water will run down the

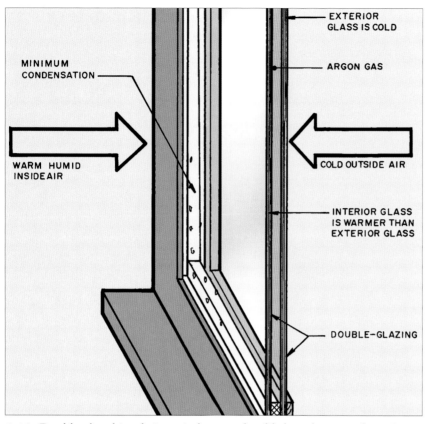

EXTERIOR GLASS IS COLD

ARGON GAS

MINIMUM CONDENSATION

WARM HUMID INSIDE AIR

COLD OUTSIDE AIR

INTERIOR GLASS IS WARMER THAN EXTERIOR GLASS

DOUBLE-GLAZING

1-10 Double-glazed insulating windows are less likely to have condensation, because the inside glass is warm.

1-11 When the glass's temperature is below the dew-point temperature and the outside air has high humidity, condensation can form on the outside of the glass.

glass and wet the frame, sill, and wall below. If it is below freezing, the moisture will freeze on the inside of the window. To help control this, put on storm windows, which provide an insulating dead-air space and reduce moisture in the air. Install ventilating fans to move moisture out of the house, especially in the kitchen and bathroom, and install a dehumidifier if the situation is very bad.

Double- and **triple-glazed windows** have an airspace between the glass panes that is usually filled with a gas, such as argon, providing insulating properties. The interior glass is therefore warmer and condensation is less likely to form (**1-10**). The frames also have insulating properties. Since insulating windows typically are warmer in the center of the glazing than around

the edges, condensation that may form will be seen on the edges.

Condensation may occur on the exterior surface of window glazing. If the glass temperature is below the dew-point temperature and the air has a high relative humidity, condensation will form (**1-11**). This most often occurs on insulated glass because the outer glass surface can have a lower temperature than the air. The **dew point** is the temperature at which air becomes saturated with water vapor and below which moisture is likely to condense. This varies with the amount of moisture in the air.

An annoying and expensive problem occurs when condensation occurs between the glasses of double-glazed windows. This is caused by the seal around the edge developing a leak. If the glazing is **factory-sealed** around the edges, leakage seldom occurs. A desiccant material in the spacer strip around the edges absorbs any moisture in the air as the unit is made and will absorb small amounts that may leak past the permanent seal. A desiccant is a drying agent such as a silica gel used between the panes of insulated glass to prevent fogging and condensation. Usually a permanent factory-sealed glazing unit will have to be replaced if it begins to fail and condense between the glass panes. Consult the manufacturer's warranty.

Some double-glazed windows use nonsealed units. These have protection around the edges but are not permanently sealed as the unit is made. If these begin to have condensation between the glasses, see whether the glazing is sealed to the sash. Some units have an air tube connecting the air between the glass panes with the outside air. This permits some air exchange and is especially helpful when the outside air is dry, which usually occurs in the winter months. Normal humidity varies with geographic location and season; so, if this glazing is chosen, consider what the usual humidity conditions are for your area.

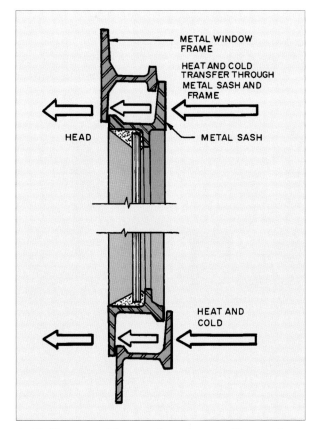

1-12 Since metal is a good conductor of heat and cold, metal frames without a thermal break will produce an energy loss. This is an example of an old steel frame.

ACOUSTIC PROPERTIES

Some windows restrict the passage of exterior sound into the house better than others. Typically a window with good air filtration and heat-loss properties will have good sound control. Sound tends to penetrate the same cracks that permit air to leak and heat to be lost.

The use of double-glazed windows will reduce the passage of sound, as will using thicker glass. See whether the window has been tested and given an **Outdoor-Indoor Transmission Class (OITC)** rating. This is a single-number rating calculated in accordance with *ASTME 1425* based on the value of the outdoor-indoor transmission loss. It provides an estimate of the performance of an exterior wall.

Sound-insulating glass also reduces sound transmission. The double-glazed glass is fixed on resilient mountings and separated so that sound is not transferred from one pane to the other. This is sometimes referred to as sound-resistive glass.

WINDOW FRAMES

Metal window frames are good conductors of heat and cold. Older metal windows conducted heat and cold into the house and even frosted up in the winter (**1-12**). This was especially a problem with alumnum window sliding doors. Newer metal windows control this problem by having thermal breaks between the outside

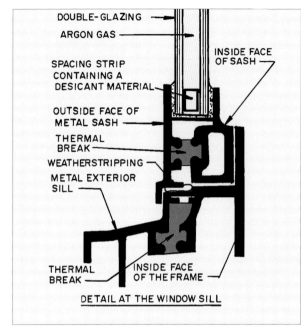

DETAIL AT THE WINDOW SILL

1-13 Metal windows with thermal breaks have a greatly reduced energy loss.

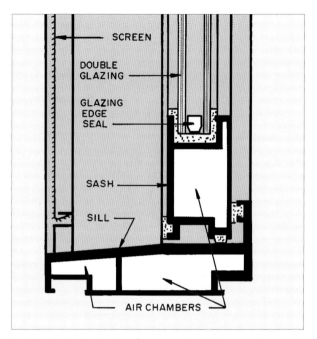

1-14 A vinyl window frame and sash has good insulation properties. Notice the dead airspaces that can be filled with foam insulation.

metal frame and the inside frame. A thermal break is a section of insulating material separating these two parts of the frame (1-13).

Vinyl frames have good insulating properties. They are made with dead-air spaces that can be filled with foam insulation to increase their insulation value. Thermal barriers may also be used (1-14). They resist the transfer of sound into the house. They are very weather resistant and do not rot, peel, or corrode.

Wood frames have excellent insulation and sound-deadening values and seldom cause condensation problems. The wood frame is pressure treated with a wood preservative. Many used today are clad in vinyl or aluminum to help resist weathering (1-15).

ULTRAVIOLET REDUCTION

The amount of ultraviolet (UV) reduction by glazing is indicated by a percentage of reduction. For example, a clear double-glazed pane may reduce UV rays by 30 to 35 percent, whereas a tinted and high-performance glaze could reduce UV by 80 percent or more.

MAINTENANCE

As windows are selected, required maintenance is a factor to consider. Vinyl and vinyl-clad wood- and aluminum-framed windows require no maintenance. An occasional washing will refresh the surface. Wood windows will require repainting after a few years. Some wood windows have a factory-applied exterior finish that is durable. Also, exterior paints are constantly being improved, and extend the life of the coating many years.

MANUFACTURER'S WARRANTY

The warranty offered by the window manufacturer is very important. It can be considered a measure of the quality of the window and how long it will last. Also check the certification label.

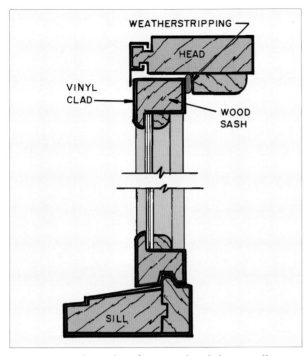

1-15 A wood window frame and sash has excellent insulating properties.

VENTILATION &
EMERGENCY EGRESS

If a window is to provide ventilation, the larger the opening the better. Double-hung and sliding windows only open half the exposed area while casement, hopper, and awning windows open the entire area. The size of the open area also determines whether the window is permitted to serve as an emergency exit in case of fire or other catastrophe. Building codes specify the minimum required openable area to the outdoors for natural ventilation. It is based on the floor area of the room. Detailed information on these codes is in Chapter 2.

BUILDING CODES

As windows are selected for type and location, the local building-code requirements must be considered. Typically these include requirements for natural light and ventilation. All habitable and occupiable rooms are required to have **natural light** providing a minimum average foot-candle illumination over the area of the room. A foot-candle is a unit of illumination equal to 1 lumen per square foot. A minimum of 6 or more foot-candles at a height of 30 inches (762mm) above the floor is typical.

All occupied spaces should have **natural ventilation** through windows, doors, louvers, or other openings. The window is generally the major source of ventilation. The area of open window area is typically specified as a percentage of the floor area of the room. An 8 to 10 percent minimum is common. When selecting windows for each room, be certain to observe your local code recommendation or requirement.

Codes also may require the use of tempered glass in areas where windows may be hit, such as near a stairway. In areas subject to specific hazards such as hurricanes, glazing resistance to penetration and wind may be specified.

Codes may have energy-performance requirements. The code may specify minimum U-factors, solar-heat-gain coefficients, and air infiltration, or may set standards for the entire house related to energy consumption. This way a very efficient insulated window will provide extra credit when determining the overall energy efficiency of the house.

Locating Windows

The location of windows in the walls of a house deserves considerable study. The choice of the type of window is important, but of even greater importance is its location, because location greatly affects the comfort of the occupants and heating and cooling costs. The location also greatly affects the exterior appearance, so that the architect has to consider both the aesthetic implications of window loation as well as its effect on the conditions inside the house.

In older houses windows are not particularly energy efficient and do not control glare, ultraviolet rays, or sound infiltration. The inefficiency of the older windows led to designers' using smaller and fewer windows, thus reducing the natural light and ventilation possibilities. However, with the high-quality energy-efficient windows today, windows can be large and plentiful. Windows, properly chosen, can be located where they provide the light, ventilation, and view desired by the home owner (2-1).

The three basic functions for windows in a house are to provide natural light, allow natural ventilation using outside air, and provide a view outdoors preferably of an attractive vista.

Courtesy Weather Shield Windows & Doors

2-1 Carefully chosen windows can provide natural light, ventilation, and a view.

NATURAL LIGHT

When people enter a room, they expect the windows to provide adequate natural light, so it should not be necessary to turn on an electric light every time the room is entered. Artificial light may be necessary for reading but not for general use of the room. The location of windows is also used to enhance interior features of the room (**2-2**) and for special needs, such as growing plants.

Natural light raises the level of illumination and therefore enhances visual comfort. The room should have balanced illumination with all areas having about the same intensity. While the eye can adjust to various levels of light intensity, try to keep the differences in a room somewhat balanced. Typical building code requirements specify a minimum average illumination of 6 foot-candles (64 lux) over the floor area of a room at a height of 30 inches (762mm) above the floor. A lux is a unit of illumination equal to 1 lumen per square meter.

The light that enters a room through a window can be balanced in many ways. The number and size of windows affect balance. The finish on the interior walls and floors is a major consider-

2-2 Windows should provide sufficient natural light so the room can be used all day without resorting to artificial light. This room uses cherry-wood-framed casement windows with transoms.

ation. A dark room can be lightened by painting the walls with a light-reflective paint. Incompatible sunny spots can be absorbed with a darker paint or curtains. Obviously a room with one window will be lighter near the window and darker across the room and in the corners. A solution is to locate several windows in the room. It is especially helpful if they can be in different walls (**2-3**). Also a skylight can bring natural light to a dark area (**2-4**).

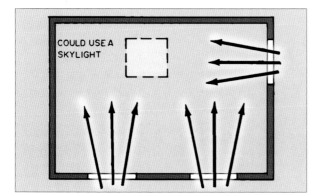

2-3 The number and location of windows is very important to provide adequate natural light. Locate windows to get a balanced overall illumination.

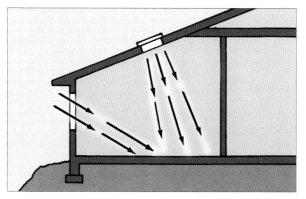

2-4 Skylights are very helpful in bringing natural light into the darker areas of a room. The resulting illumination creates a comfortable balance.

Tall, narrow windows give a narrow band of light that will go far into the room. Short, wide windows will give a wide, broad band of light. The higher the window is located on the wall, the deeper the light will penetrate into the room (**2-5**).

Remember, the natural light available varies as the sun moves through the sky. A window receiving direct rays from the sun in the morning may need to be shaded until the sun passes over

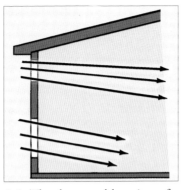

2-5 The shape and location of the window influence the band of light it will provide. High windows allow light farther into the room.

and then will provide useful, comfortable illumination the rest of the day. Notice in **2-6** that the sun strikes the east wall in the morning, flows along the south wall through the middle of the day, and moves on to the west side in the late afternoon. The north side receives very little direct sun at any time.

The angle the rays of sunlight will penetrate through a window also will vary with the seasons. In the northern hemi-

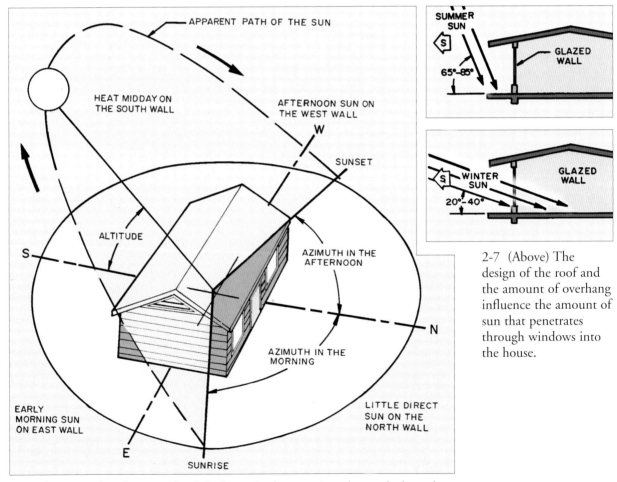

2-6 The sun strikes the east side of the house in the morning, the south through the middle of the day, and the west in late afternoon.

2-7 (Above) The design of the roof and the amount of overhang influence the amount of sun that penetrates through windows into the house.

sphere in the summer the sun is at a high angle and will strike the window steeply as compared to the lower position it appears to travel along in the winter (2-7). While this provides a degree of solar heat in the winter, it also causes some glare inside the room. Glare and deep penetration can be controlled with blinds, shades, or draperies. There are some rooms where glare and deep penetration would be undesirable, so consider window locations here carefully. Notice that the size of the roof overhang greatly influences the amount of sun penetration. In warm climates large overhangs are frequently used.

In warm southern climates in the northern hemisphere it is best to try to avoid excess exposure to the hot summer sun even though energy-efficient windows do help to reduce the heat gain. Chapter 9 has some suggestions for shielding windows in the summer.

When locating windows, consider what the exterior surroundings might do to the light. A large grass area will absorb sunlight and have little reflection. A white, sandy beach or a concrete driveway (2-8) will reflect the sun's rays and produce considerable glare through windows exposed to it. If the view is important, provide a means for temporarily blocking the glare until the sun passes over.

Skylights have slightly different characteristics than windows in the walls of a house. Once in a while the house is positioned so the rays from the sun penetrate into the house directly through the skylight (2-9). Some may find this to be as annoying as if the rays came through a window. Before planning to use skylights, check to see whether this will occur. If possible, move the skylight to another part of the roof. If this cannot be done, moveable blinds designed especially for shielding skylights are available.

Concrete driveway

Sandy beach

2-8 Some exterior surroundings will cause considerable glare through windows by reflecting the sun's rays against the wall of the house.

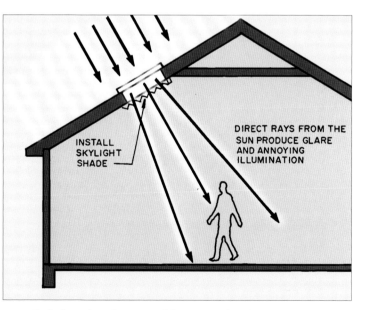
INSTALL SKYLIGHT SHADE

DIRECT RAYS FROM THE SUN PRODUCE GLARE AND ANNOYING ILLUMINATION

2-9 Skylights placed in a roof facing south will let the rays from the sun penetrate directly into the room.

Courtesy Velux-America Inc.

2-10 Properly placed skylights will provide diffused light over a wide area of a room.

They are worth the cost because this is a problem that won't go away. A northern orientation is recommended when possible. It provides a diffused light over a dark area of a room (**2-10**).

Properly positioned skylights will tend to introduce a diffused light. The light enters the glazed opening and strikes the sides of the light well leading to the ceiling. If the well is painted a light color, reflected light will be increased. If it is painted a darker color, the amount of reflected light will be decreased. Likewise the shape of the well controls the span and direction of the light distributed into the room (**2-11**).

Clerestory windows are found on some house styles. While not frequently used, they do provide another source of light. The light might be reflected off a nearby wall or extend into the room (**2-12**).

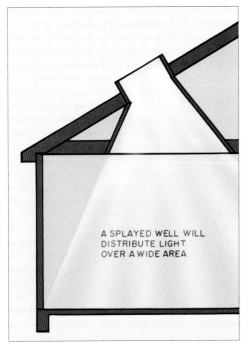

A SPLAYED WELL WILL DISTRIBUTE LIGHT OVER A WIDE AREA

2-11 The angle of the skylight well is set to let the light penetrate into the room in the area where it is needed. The sides of the well can be flared to produce a wider cone of light.

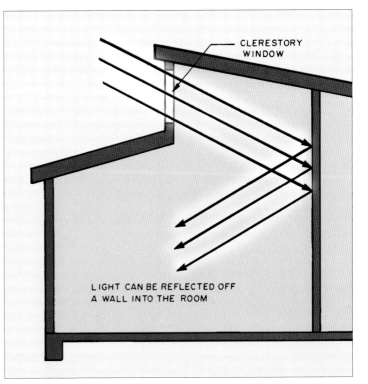

CLERESTORY WINDOW

LIGHT CAN BE REFLECTED OFF A WALL INTO THE ROOM

2-12 Clerestory windows are one way to provide increased natural illumination. They greatly influence the roof style and overall architecture of the house.

NATURAL VENTILATION

Natural ventilation increases the living quality of rooms as well as the entire house. In addition to providing fresh air, it can remove excess humidity and odors that develop.

Ventilation can be improved by locating windows away from exterior obstructions that will block airflow. Trees and shrubs planted to shield the windows from sunlight tend to reduce natural airflow (2-13).

A high-pressure air volume is created when moving air strikes the house. As the air moves across and around the house, a low-pressure area is created. Air flows from the high-pressure outside area through an open window, and across the room to the low-pressure areas on the sides of the house where there is another open window (2-14). The window opening through which the air enters the house should be smaller than the opening from which it leaves.

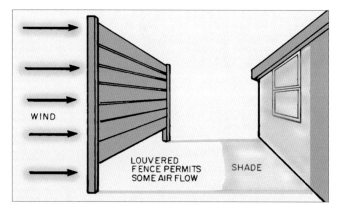

2-13 This fence shields the window from the low rays of the sun but also tends to greatly reduce the ventilation provided by the window.

Building codes generally require a room to have a minimum open-window area of eight to ten percent of the floor area. In warmer climates this minimum could well be increased.

The location of the windows controls the natural ventilation. There will be some areas in the room where the air remains stationary (2-15).

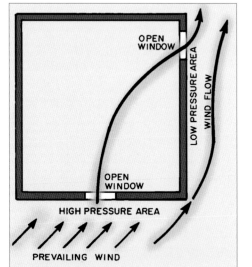

2-14 Difference in air pressure helps natural airflow into, across, and out of the room. The prevailing winds produce this flow and should be considered when windows are located.

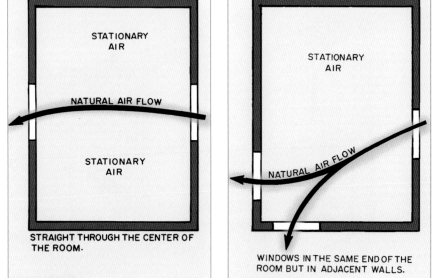

2-15 As windows are located in each room, remember to check the flow of natural ventilation. Improper placement will leave areas of stationary air within the room.

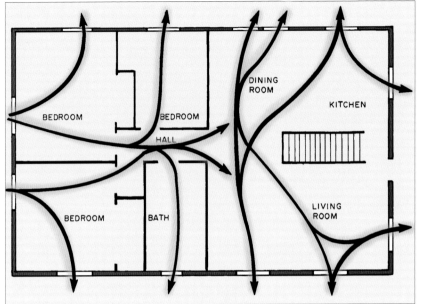

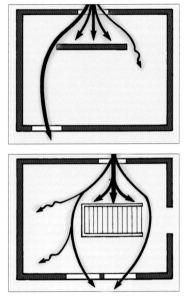

2-16 Several areas of the house can be ventilated by locating windows so natural airflow moves through the adjoining rooms.

2-17 A partition or stair can be a major obstacle, diverting or blocking the flow of air.

Planning for natural ventilation can be limited to a single room or an overall plan can be developed for airfow through several rooms or areas of the house (2-16). To provide cross-ventilation through a house, windows must be placed on all sides and positioned so that interior doors and partitions do not block the flow. Consider the direction of the prevailing winds as windows are located. When properly located, halls can also serve as means for moving natural ventilation through a house. Remember that partitions, interior doors, stairs, and other obstructions can effectively block or change the direction of airflow (2-17).

The type of window chosen also influences airflow. **Double-hung** and **sliding windows** are flush with the exterior wall and provide ventilation when the air is at lower pressure inside the room. However, only half of the total window area is open for ventilation (2-18). A **casement window** provides a full opening. In addition it can be used in the open position as a vane to direct airflow into the room (2-19). **Hopper windows** hinge on the bottom

2-18 Double-hung and sliding windows only provide one-half of their total glazed area open for natural ventilation.

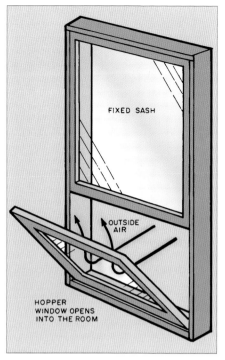

FIXED SASH

OUTSIDE AIR

HOPPER WINDOW OPENS INTO THE ROOM

FIXED SASH

OUTSIDE AIR

AWNING WINDOWS OPEN TOWARD THE OUTSIDE.

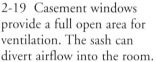

2-19 Casement windows provide a full open area for ventilation. The sash can divert airflow into the room.

2-20 A hopper window permits air to flow in from the top and protects those inside the room from having the air blow directly on them.

2-21 The awning window opens toward the exterior. Outside air can flow up into the interior room from below.

and permit some airflow over the top (**2-20**). This shields those sitting near the window from receiving the direct flow of air. **Awning windows** are hinged at the top and permit airflow from below (**2-21**). These windows can be open during rain and permit airflow.

The angle at which the air enters and leaves the room depends on the location and type of window. Airflow across the room at the level of the occupants is more comfortable than across the ceiling (**2-22**). Airflow can be adjusted by the use of hopper and awning windows (**2-23**).

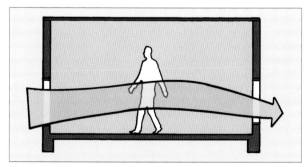

2-22 Airflow near the floor provides more comfortable conditions for those in the room than if the air were blowing across the ceiling.

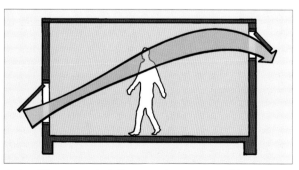

2-23 The natural airflow can be optimized by locating awning or hopper windows to take advantage of the prevailing winds.

Another excellent way to provide natural ventilation is by installing **roof windows**. A roof window is like a skylight except it can be opened (2-24). Since hot air rises, this lets out the hot, risen air and creates a path for cooler air flowing in through windows, providing ventilation. A couple of roof windows can greatly increase the overall ventilation flow for the entire house. People living in warm climates, such as in Egypt, have for hundreds of years provided an opening in the very tops of their roofs. This provides them with a measure of cooling due to natural ventilation.

As all of these factors are considered, select the style of

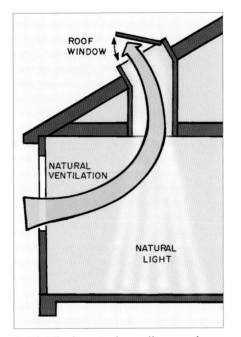

2-24 The hot air that collects at the ceiling can be vented through roof windows. It also provides a path for ventilation through the windows in the walls.

window that is appropriate for the style of the house. Also size each window to provide needed ventilation without getting it so large it compromises the exterior architecture. Two smaller windows may look better than one huge window and give you an additional chance to locate them to actually improve airflow. Remember to work to provide cross-ventilation whenever possible and to take advantage of the prevailing winds.

CONTROLLING HEAT GAIN

Heat gain can be reduced by careful window location. While new windows are more energy efficient, they still can permit some heat gain. This is especially important to consider in hot climates. Chapter 9 details some things you can do to block direct sun exposure on windows, but these often block the view and impede natural

ventilation. Of course, place the largest windows to the north. Refer back to 2-6. The east and west walls will receive fewer hours of direct sunlight than the south wall.

Reduction of the number of square feet of window area in these walls will reduce heat gain. This, however, reduces the amount of daylight and ventilation available and restricts access to any view. Choosing windows with a low solar-heat-gain coefficient is a better solution. Rather than restrict the glazing to the minimum floor-area percentage, consider installing insulated blinds or draperies for use during the hours when the sun penetration will be the greatest, and install larger windows if it is best for the rooms involved.

A window supplier can calculate the heat gain for windows to be used in sun-drenched walls. The heating/air-conditioning contractor can figure how this will affect your cooling costs.

CONTROLLING HEAT LOSS

In the winter, especially in colder climates, heating costs are a factor when locating windows. Using energy-efficient windows will provide a glazed area that has a heat-loss factor similar to many conventionally built exterior walls. The glazing will still provide some solar heat.

If cold, strong prevailing winds are predictable, it may be wise to reduce the glazing in this wall and also provide insulated blinds or draperies.

2-25 Small, high windows provide some natural light and ventilation and offer considerable privacy.

2-26 Glass blocks provide some natural light and privacy but no ventilation.

PRIVACY

Windows not only give the occupants a view of the outside world but provide some exposure of the occupants to passersby. Location can help provide some privacy. A lot depends upon the location of the house, the closeness of neighbors, and the street. Privacy may require that a window be small and located high on the wall (**2-25**). Frosted, textured, and heavily tinted glass, as well as glass and acrylic blocks, provides a measure of privacy (**2-26**). Shades and curtains can be used to provide privacy for those times when light and ventilation are not as important.

WINDOWS & FURNITURE

When planning a house, consider how the location of windows will impact on the furnishings in each room. It is suggested that scale tem-plates of furniture be cut out and positioned on the rooms on the floor plan. Examine how the proposed window location will limit the placement of furniture in the room. For example, in **2-27** the windows make it difficult to have clear wall space for a queen- or king-sized bed and to get to the window. In **2-28** there are two locations for the bed, but access to a dresser is tight.

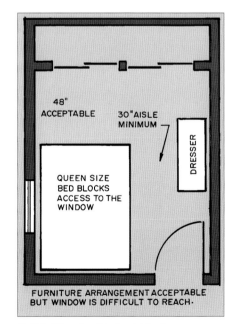

2-27 The double bed blocks access to the window, so it is difficult to open and close and adjust the blinds.

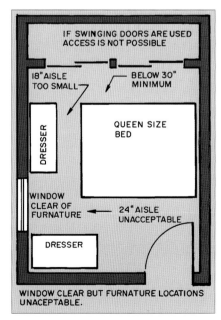

2-28 The window is accessible, but the furniture arrangement produces unacceptable aisles.

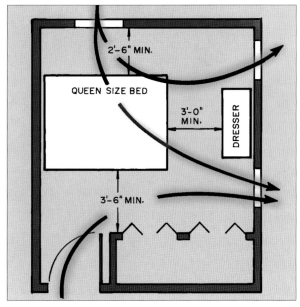

2-29 This bedroom has several accessible windows and room for the desired furniture. It has adequate natural light, and ventilation is satisfactory. The minimum recommended spaces between furniture and walls are shown. Could the bed be located in another place and still maintain the minimum spacing?

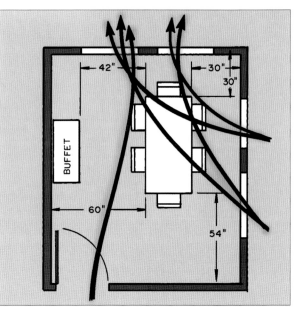

2-30 This dining room provides minimum room for the furniture and has plenty of natural light and ventilation. Try to rearrange the furniture and maintain the minimum spacing shown.

2-31 The large expanse of windows provides an excellent view of a river from the living area of the home.

Courtesy Weather Shield Windows & Doors

A bedroom layout with ample room is shown in **2-29**. There is room for the table, chairs, and a buffet with windows providing plenty of light and ventilation in the dining room in **2-30**.

VIEWS

Many residential lots are chosen because they border on an area providing an attractive view. While most sites cannot view the ocean or mountains in the distance, other possibilities exist such as a golf course, river, patio, or dense woods (**2-31**). While the view may be in a direction that produces hot sun

2-32 An attractive garden or patio can be the focus of attention outside a large glass wall area.

Courtesy Weather Shield Windows & Doors

2-33 This series of casement and fixed windows frames a view of the exterior plantings.

in the summer or heavy winds and snow in the winter, these can be handled as explained in this chapter. Since any climate problems can be worked out later, your first consideration should be a nice view.

Select and locate windows connecting the outside with the inside. Japanese homes take advantage of inner gardens that are surrounded by the house to create some form of courtyard (**2-32**).

The size of the windows depends upon how they look from the exterior. Windows need to be in balance with the exterior mass of the house. The location is of major importance. Place windows so they frame the best part of the view (**2-33**). If there is some unfortunate, unattractive area nearby, try to block it out of the view by the location and size of the window used.

Remember, large windows permit intrusion on privacy, so provide for enclosure whenever it is needed.

Consider whether a large, unobstructed glazing area is wanted or if a window with small glass panes is preferred (**2-34**). Large glass areas provide an unobstructed view, while small panes tend to obscure it. The choice also involves the architectural design of the exterior of the house.

1. SMALL PANES GLASS MAKE VIEWING A SCENE DIFFICULT.

2. LARGER GLASS AREAS MAKE IT EASIER TO ENJOY THE VIEW.

3. A SINGLE GLAZED AREA PROVIDES THE BEST VIEW.

2-34 The choice of glazing directly influences the ease of viewing an exterior scene.

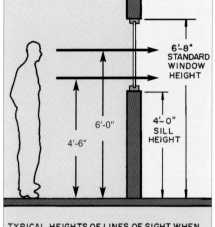

2-35 High windows give some privacy while providing a view outside when a person is standing. Lines of sight shown are for persons 5'-1" to 6'-3" tall using typical-height furniture.

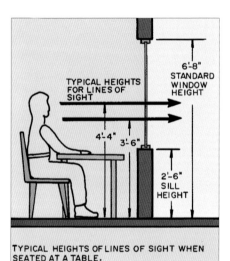

2-36 Windows to provide a view for those seated at a table should have a sill low enough to provide a direct line of sight. Lines of sight shown are for persons 5'-1" to 6'-3" tall using typical-height furniture.

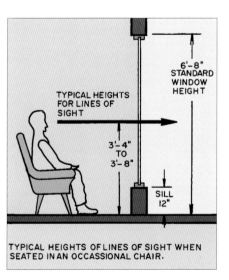

2-37 Large glass windows usually have a very low sill and are often placed where those viewing the exterior are seated in comfortable upholstered chairs. Lines of sight shown are for persons 5'-1" to 6'-3" tall using typical-height furniture.

Locate windows so that the line of sight to a view is not obstructed. Sills and horizontal members should be kept out of the line of sight. The position of the person viewing—as well as whether a typical viewer will be standing or seated, and the kind of seating—may affect the optimal window positioning. Notice in **2-35** that when a person is standing the line of sight is typically 4 feet, 8 inches to 6 feet. This means a high window should have sills no higher than 4 feet. Likewise, when one is seated at a table, a 2-feet, 6-inch sill is about as high as is desirable (**2-36**). Large picture windows typically run close to the floor and have the sill 6 to10 inches (152 to 254mm) above the floor (**2-37**).

SECURITY

Window size and location have an impact on security. First find out what hardware is on the window to prevent unwanted entrance. If security could be a problem, consider the use of narrow, high windows. They let in some light and ventilation but do offer protection. Some windows have hardware that will allow them to be opened only two or three inches. This permits some ventilation yet is secure. However, refer to codes for requirements for egress.

Windows that face porches, decks, and patios or that are close to the ground present greater security risks than those well above the ground (**2-38**).

2-38 Windows on porches, decks, or close to the ground are security risks and require special attention.

EMERGENCY EXITS

Most building codes require each bedroom to have one operable window or an exterior door to serve as an emergency exit. The window should be able to be opened from the inside without a special tool. The sill is usually required to be not more than 44 inches (1118mm) above the floor. The egress opening for bedroom windows on the first floor is typically specified as 5.0 ft² (0.47m²), and for windows on the second floor, 5.7 ft² (0.53m²). This opening is large enough for a fireman with an airpack to enter.

Codes typically require the opening to be at least 20 inches (559mm) wide and 24 inches (610mm) high. These are the minimum sizes for the sides of the actual opening, not the manufacturer's stated window unit size (2-39).

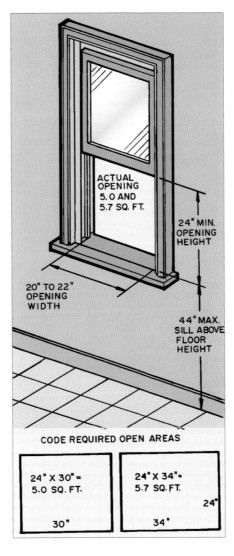

ACTUAL OPENING 5.0 AND 5.7 SQ. FT.

24" MIN. OPENING HEIGHT

20" TO 22" OPENING WIDTH

44" MAX. SILL ABOVE FLOOR HEIGHT

CODE REQUIRED OPEN AREAS

24" X 30" = 5.0 SQ. FT.
30"

24" X 34" = 5.7 SQ. FT.
24"
34"

However, a 22 x 24-inch window opening only provides 3.3 ft² of opening.

To meet the 5.0 and 5.7 ft² requirement, the actual opening will have to be 24 x 30 inches to provide 5.0 ft² and 24 x 34 inches to provide 5.7 ft² of clear opening. Consider which window will be the emergency exit, and see what conditions will exist on the outside as a person exits and drops to the ground. Some codes permit exits to be up to 20 feet above the ground, which is quite a drop. Be certain to review your local code for specific requirements.

2-39 These are typical requirements for a window opening to serve as a means of emergency egress. Check your local code for requirements.

CHAPTER 3

Types of Window

Window manufacturers have available a wide range of window types made from several materials. As you consider which windows to use, also consider the purposes they are to serve. These are covered in detail in Chapters 1 and 2. Notice some provide only natural light. Others can provide an expansive view of a pleasant scene (**3-1**). Ventilation provided by some window types is limited, but the natural ventilation can be somewhat directed by the sash. Other types open fully, and 100 percent of the opening is available for natural ventilation. If you need to provide emergency egress, very few window types will meet this code requirement. Consider this as the type of window is selected (**Table 3-1**).

WINDOW-FRAME MATERIALS

For many years window units were made from wood. While these served very well, and continue to do so, other materials are currently finding increasing use. Among these are composite wood products, fiberglass, and vinyl. These all are strong, resist weathering better than wood, and allow for the use of narrower profiles. This makes the glazed area a bit larger than the typical wood window of the same size.

The window-frame material affects the energy efficiency of windows because it tends to draw heat away from the edges of the glass. This is why frost forms on the edges of the glass in cold weather. The edges are colder.

Courtesy Weather Shield Windows & Doors

3-1 Fixed windows provide an unobstructed view and admit considerable natural light.

TABLE 3-1 TYPES OF WINDOW COMMONLY USED IN RESIDENTIAL CONSTRUCTION

Acrylic-block	Custom-made	Roof window
Awning	Garden	Single-, double-,
Bow	Glass-block	and triple-hung
Bay	Grill	Skylight
Casement	Hopper/utility	Sliding
Circle-top, arched,	Fixed	Storm
quarter-circle, circle,	Jalousie	Tilt
elliptical, and oval	Replacement	Transom

WOOD FRAMES

Wood frames have been the standard for many years. They are good insulators and are energy efficient. The wood frame and sash are treated with water-repellent preservatives and are factory-primed, providing an excellent base for the exterior paint. Manufacturers offer wood frames that are clad with vinyl or aluminum that is maintenance free (3-2).

VINYL FRAMES

Vinyl frames are widely used in the manufacture of replacement windows and windows used in new construction. They are lightweight and operate well. They require little maintenance and will not swell when exposed to moisture. Low-density cellular vinyl frames have the same thermal resistance as solid wood. Those made with cavities filled with foam insulation have a higher thermal resistance than wood.

FIBERGLASS FRAMES

Fiberglass frames will not shrink, warp, swell, or rot. They are strong and can hold larger fixed panes of glass. They have the best thermal resistance of all types of frame. Those made with

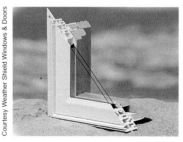

3-2 This wood frame and sash is clad with extruded PVC vinyl. It provides a maintenance-free surface that eliminates the need for painting.

internal cavities filled with insulation have an even higher R-value. Fiberglass frames have a coefficient of thermal expansion close to glass, which reduces stress on the glass and frame.

ALUMINUM FRAMES

Aluminum frames require little maintenance, are lightweight, and operate easily. Exposure to moisture does not cause them to swell. They generally have poor insulation properties. However, some types are made with insulating thermal breaks between the inside and outside parts of the frame and sash. This greatly improves their thermal resistance. They have colors electrostatically bonded to the aluminum surface, providing a fade-resisting coating.

WOOD-COMPOSITE FRAMES

A wood-composite frame is made from shredded, dried, seasoned hardwoods mixed with resins and preservatives and fused under heat and pressure. A wood-composite frame looks a lot like wood. It has good thermal resistance and is dimensionally stable. Since it is prefinished during manufacture, it does not require painting.

SINGLE- ,DOUBLE- & TRIPLE-HUNG WINDOWS

Hung-type windows have sash that move in a vertical direction. They are counterbalanced by some type of mechanism. This holds them in the open position regardless of the amount of opening. Hung windows provide an opening for natural ventilation, and the sash does not project outward or inward when open. Only part of the total window allows ventilation (**3-3**).

A **single-hung window** has a fixed upper sash, and the lower sash slides up over it (**3-4**). **Double-hung windows** have both sash moving in a vertical position (**3-5**). This permits arranging them so ventilation can occur through the open bottom or top sash or split with some coming from each area. In each case less than 50 percent of the total window is open. **Triple-hung windows** are used where a larger glazed opening is required, providing more light. They will also provide more ventilation than **double-hung windows**. All three sash move vertically, allowing air to enter at the top, center, or bottom of the window opening (**3-6**).

Double-hung windows (sometimes called vertical-sliding windows) may have single panes of glass (**3-7**) or be divided into small panes. Those divided into small panes have vertical and horizontal muntins into which the glass fits (**3-8**). For ease of cleaning and reduced cost the sash may have a single glass with a divider over it, giving the appearance of a divided-light window.

Hardware for hung windows includes locks on the meeting rails and sometimes a sash lift on the bottom rail. **Sash locks** provide a minimum of security and pull the meeting rails of each sash together, closing them tightly against the weather stripping. This effectively reduces air infiltration.

WOOD HUNG

VINYL-CLAD WOOD HUNG

Courtesy Marvin Windows and Doors

3-3 These are wood double-hung windows with a wood frame and sash. The sash on these examples tilt in for easy cleaning.

SINGLE-HUNG

3-4 Only the bottom sash moves on a single-hung window. The upper sash remains fixed. Thus ventilation is only possible through the opening produced by sliding the lower sash up over the fixed sash.

DOUBLE-HUNG

3-5 Both sash move vertically on double-hung windows—also called "vertical sliding windows." They can be adjusted to permit air to enter at the top or bottom or at both places at the same time.

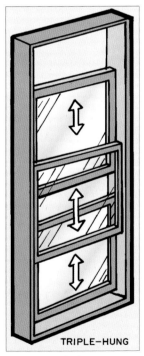

TRIPLE-HUNG

3-6 A triple-hung window is larger and provides more natural light and ventilation.

3-7 These double-hung windows are glazed with a single glass pane in each sash.

3-8 This double-hung window has the glazed area divided into small lights.

Hung windows are held open with a spiral balance or compression-type jamb-liner sash slide. The **spiral balance** is a tube, a coiled spring, and a spiral rod (**3-9**). If the sash will not stay open or will not stay closed, the tension on the spring will have to be adjusted. To do this, remove the tube from the frame but do not let the screw come out of the tube (**3-10**). If the spring is too tight, turn the tube with the screw a couple turns counterclockwise. If the sash is hard to move or will not stay open, tighten the spring a couple turns clockwise. Reinstall the tube on the frame. Hung windows will have a balance on each side.

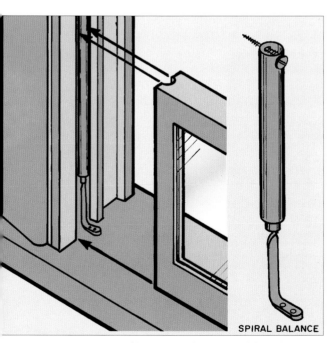

SPIRAL BALANCE

3-9 Some types of hung window are held in the open position by a spring-loaded spiral balance.

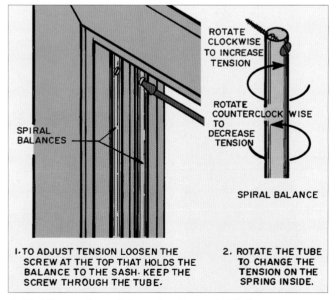

SPIRAL BALANCES

ROTATE CLOCKWISE TO INCREASE TENSION

ROTATE COUNTERCLOCKWISE TO DECREASE TENSION

SPIRAL BALANCE

1. TO ADJUST TENSION LOOSEN THE SCREW AT THE TOP THAT HOLDS THE BALANCE TO THE SASH. KEEP THE SCREW THROUGH THE TUBE.

2. ROTATE THE TUBE TO CHANGE THE TENSION ON THE SPRING INSIDE.

3-10 The tension of the spring in a spiral balance can be adjusted by loosening it from the frame and turning it clockwise to increase the tension and counterclockwise to reduce it.

A **compression jamb-liner sash slide** is made of high-impact polyvinyl chloride or aluminum. The compression jamb liner has a springlike quality that presses against the sides of the sash, holding it in place by pressure (**3-11**). It also effectively seals off air infiltration around the edges of the sash.

Hung windows can be mounted as single units, or in groups of two or three or more (**3-12**). They are separated by a mullion—the vertical framing member separating windows that are set in a series. Hung windows are also set on each side of a large fixed window, providing a wide glazed area and permitting some ventilation (**3-13**).

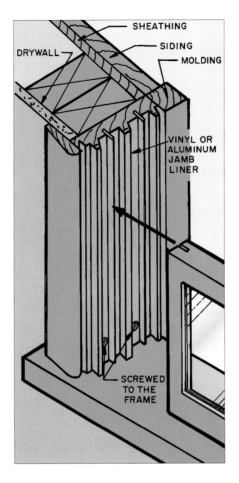

SHEATHING
DRYWALL
SIDING
MOLDING
VINYL OR ALUMINUM JAMB LINER
SCREWED TO THE FRAME

Window screens are located on the outside of the unit so they do not interfere with opening the sash.

CASEMENT WINDOWS

Casement windows have the sash hinged on the vertical side and generally swing toward the exterior (**3-14**). Swing-in units are available but they project into the room and become obstacles. The sash are swung open and

3-11 Some hung windows control the sash movement with a compression jamb-liner sash slide. This is just one design. Many others are available.

3-12 Hung windows are frequently installed in groups of two or more, providing a wide expanse of glass and considerable natural ventilation. They are separated by a mullion. This installation has an elliptical window over it. The top sash has bars applied, creating the appearance of small panes of glass.

pulled closed by a crank mechanism (**3-15**). When closed, the sash are pulled tight against the weather stripping and secured by several locks (**3-16**). Average-sized windows have a lock near the top and bottom of the sash while large windows will have a third lock in the center.

Casement windows provide ventilation through the entire window opening. The open casement sash can act as a vane, catching and directing passing wind into the room.

SINGLE CASEMENT DOUBLE CASEMENT

3-14 Casement windows are hinged on one side and swing out, providing the entire opening with ventilation.

3-13 This window unit has a large fixed center sash with hung windows on each side. The quarter-round, circle-top, and transom units on the top reflect the shape of the gable end.

3-15 A typical cranking mechanism used to open and close the sash on casement windows.

3-16 The sash is locked to the frame, sealing it against the weather stripping. This is a lever-type lock that pulls the sash and frame together.

3-17 This double casement window provides a large glazed area and when open provides considerable natural ventilation. Notice the transom windows on top, which provide additional natural light.

3-18 This installation of multiple single-casement windows with transom windows provides a dramatic view of the exterior as well as natural light and ventilation. The windows are separated by mullions.

In very windy weather casement windows will be buffeted by the wind; so, if they are left open, they could be damaged. They do present an obstacle if a sidewalk is close to the house.

Swing-out casements have the screen on the inside. The opening handle is below the screen and does not interfere with opening the sash.

Casement windows can be installed as single or double units. The double unit has a right- and a left-swinging sash that meet on a rail in the center (**3-17**). Casement windows also can be

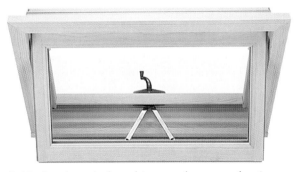

3-19 Awning windows hinge at the top and swing out. This allows ventilation even during light rains.

mounted in multiple units (**3-18**). Another type of unit has a fixed sash in the center and casement windows on each side. Casement windows are also used on other types of window unit such as bay and bow windows.

AWNING WINDOWS

Awning windows are hinged at the top and project outside the house (**3-19**). The sash is opened and closed with a cranking mechanism. The sash is locked with a sash lock that pulls it firmly against the weather stripping. The screen is on the inside of the unit but the cranking handle is below the screen, enabling the sash to be opened.

Awning windows provide protection of the opening during normal rains, so allow ventilation to continue when other types of window would have to be closed.

Awning windows are available in single, double, and triple units (**3-20**). They also are used in combination with other types of window (**3-21**).

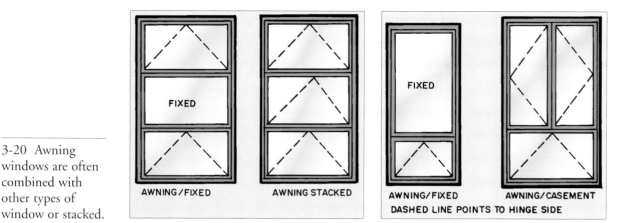

3-20 Awning windows are often combined with other types of window or stacked.

AWNING/FIXED

AWNING STACKED

FIXED

AWNING/FIXED

AWNING/CASEMENT

DASHED LINE POINTS TO HINGE SIDE

HOPPER/UTILITY WINDOWS

Hopper windows are about the same as awning windows. However, they are hinged at the bottom and project into the room (**3-22**). In residential construction they are often used for basement windows. When open, the windows tilt in from the top, providing ventilation that does not blow directly on the occupants in the room.

These windows are used in many commercial buildings, such as schools and office buildings, where ventilation is wanted but the occupants do not want the air blowing directly on them. In the open position they provide only limited protection from the rain. Since they open in, they are easy to clean from the inside. When screens are used, they are placed on the outside.

Courtesy Weather Shield Windows & Doors

3-21 A large fixed sash has awning windows below to provide natural ventilation to this picture window.

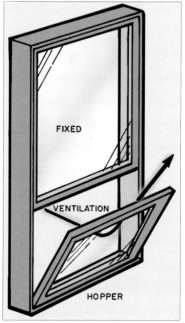

3-22 Hopper windows open into the room and divert air upward. They can be installed with other types of window.

Hopper windows have a lock operated by a handle. This pulls the sash tight against the weather stripping. To open the window, unlock it and pull in on the handle.

In basement construction hopper windows are generally mounted as individual units and spaced along the basement wall as required. They can be butted and installed as multiple units, provided the structural framing over them will carry the floor load. In wall construction, units are frequently stacked or combined with other windows.

NORMAL POSITION ADJUSTED FOR EASY CLEANING

3-23 Tilt windows make it easy to clean both sides of the sash from inside the house.

TILT WINDOWS

One type of tilt window is shown in **3-23**. This is a double-hung window operating like any standard double-hung window. However, it has a special patented system that allows each sash to tilt out of the frame, permitting easy cleaning.

FIXED WINDOWS

A fixed window is used to provide natural illumination in an area where natural ventilation is not needed. A typical application is to provide a view of a great scene, such as the mountains or the ocean (**3-1**). There are a number of units available in a wide range of sizes. They are also used in connection with other windows as shown in **3-20**, and they are mounted permanently in the frame. Since many are large, a strong frame and sash are required. Usually energy-efficient insulating glazing is used, otherwise the heat loss and gain would be considerable.

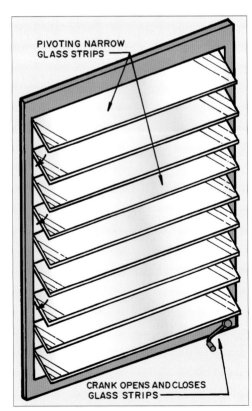

PIVOTING NARROW GLASS STRIPS

CRANK OPENS AND CLOSES GLASS STRIPS

JALOUSIE WINDOWS

Jalousie windows have a series of glass louvers covering the window opening (**3-24**). When open, they appear much like the louvers used to ventilate an attic. They do not seal very tightly and will admit some air even when

3-24 Jalousie windows have a glazed area made of many narrow strips of glass that rotate to provide ventilation. Because they are not energy efficient, they are not used as windows opening into the interior of a house.

closed, but they do keep out rain. They are typically used to enclose porches to keep them dry, and to protect them from the wind, yet be able to be opened when the weather is nice, providing a wide-open area for natural ventilation. The view through these windows is not good even when they are open. If an unobstructed view of the yard or something in the distance is wanted, try a different type of window.

If in very hot or very cold weather additional protection is needed, install interior storm windows, which can be removed during fair weather. Some types come with screens that can replace the storm windows.

The glass louvers have metal clips on the ends and a pivot pin that enters the window frame. Each louver pivots on its own pin. The louvers are connected to a crank mechanism that rotates all of them horizontally simultaneously.

GLIDING WINDOWS

The sash on gliding windows move horizontally on a track (**3-25**). These units are available in a number of assemblies. One type has a fixed sash over which a sliding sash moves. This permits half of the total window to be opened for ventilation, but only on one side. Another type

Courtesy Andersen Windows, Inc.

3-25 A wood-framed gliding window. One sash moves horizontally, providing ventilation through half the total unit size.

has both sash able to slide. This permits an adjustment as to which side provides ventilation, but still limits the opening to half the total window area (**3-26**).

With this window the sash stays in the plane of the wall so there is no projection into the room or outside. It has a locking latch securing each sliding sash. Screens are installed on the outside. Some types permit the sash to be removed for easy cleaning.

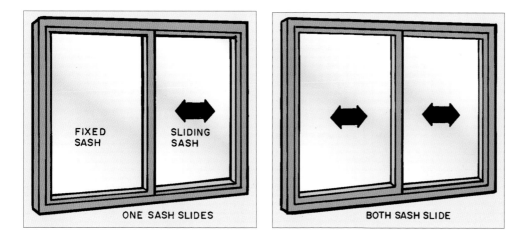

FIXED SASH   **SLIDING SASH**

ONE SASH SLIDES

BOTH SASH SLIDE

3-26 Typical gliding windows. Some have one sash move and others both sash move.

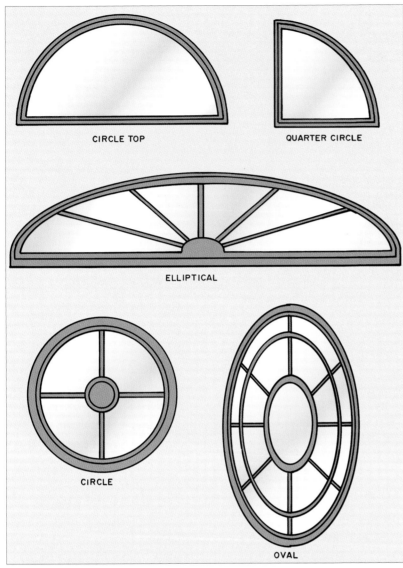

3-27 Typical profiles for special windows having circular features.

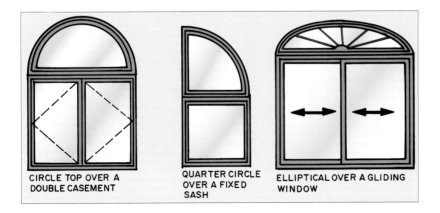

CIRCLE-TOP, ARCHED, QUARTER-CIRCLE, CIRCLE, ELLIPTICAL & OVAL WINDOWS

Typical profiles for these windows are in **3-27**. The circle-top, quarter-circle, and elliptical windows are generally mounted on top of another type of window such as a casement or hung window (**3-28**). A circle-top window over a fixed sash with two casements is in **3-29**. The elliptical-top window in **3-30** adds to the architectural appearance of the total window installation. Circle-top and elliptical windows are also installed over doors.

Circle and oval windows are mounted as individual units (**3-31**). They have the glass permanently secured in the frame and so supply light but no ventilation. They are generally double glazed and made with the flashing shaped to the contour of the unit.

Another circle top is shown in **3-32**. These windows are used as focal points in the architecture of the building. They admit considerable light and are frequently used to

3-28 Circle-top, quarter-circle, and elliptical windows are usually installed above other types of window.

Courtesy Weather Shield Windows & Doors

3-29 This circle-top window admits additional light and is an attractive architectural feature. Notice the use of gothic grills overlaid on all the windows.

Courtesy Weather Shield Windows & Doors

3-30 This installation has an elliptical window crowning the assembly of windows.

Courtesy Weather Shield Windows & Doors

3-31 This circle window provides light into the area and is an important architectural feature of the room.

provide natural light in an entrance hall or foyer. They are available in a range of widths and heights. Threel are shown in **3-33**. They are fixed units, so these do not provide ventilation.

An arch-type fixed window is shown in **3-34**. It is used to provide a significant view of the exterior and admits considerable natural light. Some arch-type windows are permanently mounted in the frame and provide no ventilation, while other designs are built around casement windows, so that the window assembly can provide both light and ventilation.

Courtesy Weather Shield Windows & Doors

3-32 This large variation of a circle-top window spans the fixed center window and the two side casements. It admits considerable light into the bathroom.

3-33 This variation of a circle-top window provides a large glazed area.

Courtesy Weather Shield Windows & Doors

3-34 Arch-type windows have an elliptical top providing a focal point on an assembly of windows.

CUSTOM-MADE WINDOWS

Some manufacturers will custom-build windows to fit the desired openings. Windows shaped as triangles, trapezoids, pentagons, hexagons, octagons, and parallelograms are typical examples. These have fixed glazing, so provide light but no ventilation.

BOW WINDOW   BAY WINDOW

3-35 Bow and bay windows extend out beyond the exterior wall and provide a focal point for the wall.

BOW & BAY WINDOWS

Bow and bay windows' primary purpose is to add a bit of architectural design to the exterior of the house. A plain, flat wall with standard windows is enhanced by using a bow or bay window instead (3-35). These also add an attractive feature to the inside because they provide a recessed area that has many decorating possibilities (3-36). In addition they provide a greater view of the exterior scene.

A **bay window** is a three-window prefabricated unit with the center unit parallel with the wall of the house and the side windows on an angle of 30 degrees or 45 degrees to the exterior wall (3-37). The center window may be fixed or operable, and the side windows are operable. Casement and double-hung windows are used. The windows are joined with mullions and the entire thing is held together with a headboard and a seatboard (3-38). It is shipped assembled, ready for installation.

Since the window cantilevers beyond the floor and roof, some means of protecting the headboard from the weather is required. It may be covered by the roof overhang and sealed to it, or a separate roof may be built over the unit. Refer to Chapter 6. A copper roof provides a special attractiveness to the installation.

A **bow window** is much the same as the bay window except it is built following a gentle outward curving arc (3-39). This is typically an angle of 10 degrees. Bow windows are available in sizes containing three to seven sash. The longer the unit, the farther it cantilevers beyond the outside wall. The bow window will have several sash that open, and these are usually casement type. The rest have the same sash as the casement but are fixed.

3-36 Bow and bay windows provide a place for attractive decoration as well as natural light and ventilation.

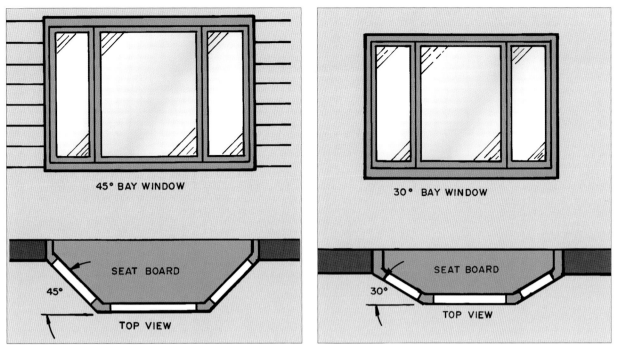

45° BAY WINDOW

SEAT BOARD

45°

TOP VIEW

30° BAY WINDOW

SEAT BOARD

30°

TOP VIEW

3-37 A bay window has three sides and the assembled unit extends out beyond the exterior wall of the house.

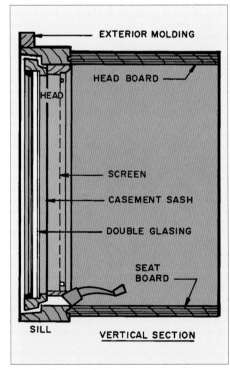

EXTERIOR MOLDING

HEAD BOARD

HEAD

SCREEN

CASEMENT SASH

DOUBLE GLASING

SEAT BOARD

SILL

VERTICAL SECTION

3-38 The windows on bay and bow window units are assembled around a headboard and a seatboard.

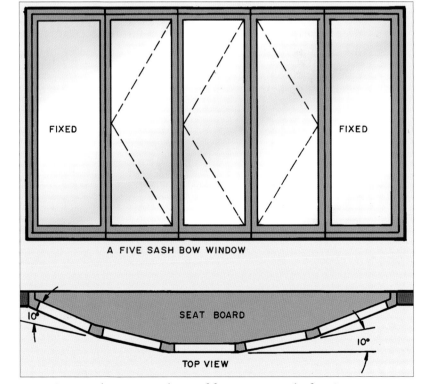

FIXED

FIXED

A FIVE SASH BOW WINDOW

SEAT BOARD

10°

10°

TOP VIEW

3-39 Bay windows are made up of five or seven sash, forming an arc. They extend outside the exterior wall of the house.

TYPES OF WINDOW   41

3-40 Transom windows are mounted above doors or windows. They provide additional light and an interesting architectural feature.

3-41 Removable grilles are an attractive architectural feature.

TRANSOM WINDOWS

A transom window is a single sash mounted above a door or window. It provides additional light, and those that are operable permit limited ventilation. Window manufacturers make these using the same design as their regular windows so the transom window fits smoothly into the overall appearance of the installation (3-40).

GRILLES

Some window manufacturers provide a variety of removable perimeter grilles (3-41). They are made of wood to match the wood on the interior of the window. Pine, oak, maple, and cherry are available. The grilles snap in and out of the frame. This makes it easy to clean the window.

3-42 A box bay window provides a place to grow plants.

BOX BAY WINDOWS

Box bay windows (also called garden windows) are used in place of standard windows to provide a lighted, shelved area in which to grow plants (3-42). The structural frame supports a sloped glazed roof and a fixed sash on the outside. The box structure juts out from the outside wall of the house. The end panels may be operable. Casement windows are often used for the end panels. The sash of the casement ends crank open and closed and have full screens.

The unit is secured to the rough opening in the wall and flashed much like other windows. The seatboard is insulated and the glazing is typically double-glazed insulating glass. Units are available typically from 36 inches to 60 inches square.

Courtesy Velux-America, Inc.

3-43 Skylights provide considerable natural lighting and open up the room visually.

Courtesy Velux-America, Inc.

3-44 A balcony roof window provides a lot of natural light, a view, and natural ventilation.

ROOF WINDOWS/ SKYLIGHTS

The terms "roof window" and "skylight" are often used interchangeably; however, there is a distinct difference. A **roof window** is a glazed unit mounted on a roof to admit natural light and can be opened to provide ventilation. A **skylight** is a glazed unit mounted on a roof that admits natural light but does not open (**3-43**). Additional information is in Chapter 8.

A unique application is a balcony roof window (**3-44**). It makes it possible to open up an attic space. The top sash opens to provide ventilation and pivots inward so it is easy to clean. The sash opens outward, forming a balcony railing when it is open (**3-45**). Skylights provide considerable natural light and an interesting architectural feature during the day and at night.

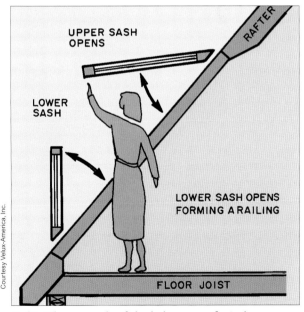

Courtesy Velux-America, Inc.

3-45 The top sash of the balcony roof window open up. The lower sash is hinged on the bottom and swings out, forming a balcony rail.

REPLACEMENT WINDOWS

As windows in older homes deteriorate, attempts can be made to repair them by replacing rotted parts, restringing those with sash balances that run over a pulley, or patch rotted wood with a wood filler. After all of this the window is still old and not energy efficient. It is far better to replace these units with one of the replacement windows available from window manufacturers. They are typically vinyl-framed units with energy-efficient glass and operating systems as well as weather stripping to effectively stop air infiltration. In Chapter 7 several types of replacement window are shown and installation procedures discussed.

3-46 Glass blocks are made by bonding two halves that have cavities. This forms a dead airspace in the block.

GLASS-BLOCK WINDOWS

Glass blocks are made by fusing two formed glass halves together. Most types have a hollow space in the center that has a partial vacuum (3-46). While they are strong and have good compressive strength, they are not used to carry a load as is possible with a solid masonry wall. They have good thermal insulation properties approaching that of double-glazed windows. They have zero air infiltration and offer a high degree of security (3-47).

Glass blocks are available in a variety of shapes. Those most frequently used are square. The most commonly used sizes are 6, 8, and 12 inches long and 2, 3, and 4 inches thick. Several installation systems are offered by manufacturers, including an aluminum framing system, a system using plastic channels, and concrete mortar similar to that used to lay bricks. See Chapter 5 for more details.

3-47 This glass-block window admits natural light, yet protects the privacy of those in the room.

Glass blocks are available with a wide range of surface finishes. They range from a clear block through blocks with various degrees of surface texture and patterns. Some block the view and provide a great deal of privacy while admitting natural light, while others permit some visual exposure. Glass blocks with light color tints make it possible to coordinate the window and light with the colors used to decorate the room. Some colors available are peach, gold, blue, gray, and green.

While glass blocks do not permit ventilation, they can be combined with other windows or doors as shown in **3-48**.

Various glass-block units and their method of assembly together with the size of the window have fire ratings of 45, 60, and 90 minutes. The manufacturers have information on their products and indicate the tests used to achieve the ratings they advertise. Check to see whether these ratings apply to both masonry and wood-framed walls.

3-48 Glass blocks are used as side lights for this residential entrance.

ACRYLIC-BLOCK WINDOWS

Acrylic-block window units are made from lightweight acrylic blocks that are connected by resilient polymer clips, and set into complete window units (**3-49**). The acrylic blocks are hermetically sealed to help reduce condensation and have an airspace that increases their energy efficiency. Pre-assembled panels have nailing fins, so they are installed in the same manner as other types of window. The blocks are available in 6- and 8-inch squares.

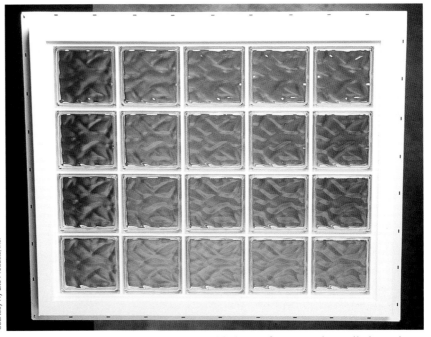

3-49 Acrylic-block windows are assembled into frames and installed much like other windows.

3-50 These acrylic-block windows are installed as fixed units, admitting light but allowing no ventilation.

Acrylic-block preassembled window units are available in fixed (**3-50**), casement (**3-51**), arch-top (**3-52**), awning, and circle-top units. They can also be custom made to the architect's design. Several surface patterns are available as well as a range of colors. The aluminum and vinyl frames are also available in several colors.

STORM WINDOWS

Storm windows are installed over existing windows that, while in good condition, are not energy efficient. The storm window reduces air infiltration and creates a dead-air space, providing some energy saving. When installed on the outside of the existing window, a storm window also protects it from weathering. Storm windows with low-E glazing increase the energy-saving properties. Tilt-in sash used on the inside of the existing windows make storm windows easy to clean. In all cases storm windows help reduce noise transmission and provide an additional measure of security.

Generally storm windows are framed with aluminum, which is strong and provides a window with a relatively narrow frame (**3-53**). They are best installed over existing wood windows. The wood window frame provides a thermal break, reducing the transfer of heat and cold through the aluminum. Some prefer not to install storm windows over vinyl frames because the higher temperatures between the units cause greater expansion and contraction of the frames. If installed over aluminum-

3-51 This casement window is glazed with acrylic blocks. They are lightweight and provide privacy.

Courtesy Hy-Lite Products, Inc.

3-52 Acrylic blocks can be fit to arch- and circle-top sash. This arch-top acrylic-block window unit complements the architectural arch in the room.

3-53 This aluminum-framed storm window was installed over wood double-hung windows, increasing energy efficiency and providing a degree of security.

framed windows, a gasket such as cork should separate them so each can expand and contract at its own rate.

Storm windows are available for installation on the outside or inside of the existing windows. They may be a single fixed unit, or be sliding units moving either vertically or horizontally. Some types have screens that allow the existing window to be open and the glazed sash of the storm window to be open, permitting natural ventilation. Screen material may be aluminum, which is strong but can corrode and dent. Fiberglass screen is less expensive and, while it will not dent, it does tear easily and stretches if pressed. Additional information is given in Chapter 7.

Energy-Efficiency Factors

As plans you make for the design or re-modeling of a house, windows are a major feature. They not only influence the appearance but are a major factor as energy efficiency of the design is considered. High-quality energy-efficient windows cost more than lower-cost units but will save enough on the utility bills to pay for themselves in a few years. After that the savings continue for years ahead. In addition, higher-quality windows are better constructed from higher-quality materials and will have reduced maintenance costs. Moreover, the house will be more comfortable in all seasons (4-1).

CHOOSING THE RIGHT WINDOW

The choice of window is influenced by the geographic location of the house. The windows in northern climates must be effective in maintaining the heat within the house and excluding the penetration of the exterior cold temperatures. In the southern climates the windows need primarily to exclude heat gain from the high outside air temperature and sun. Windows in the central states need to balance heat gain and loss because the exterior temperatures typically do not reach the extremes of the North and South and not for extended periods. Therefore the main concern is the need to keep the heat in or out of the house depending upon the season.

Courtesy Weather Shield Windows & Doors

4-1 These energy-efficient windows are used in new construction. They greatly reduce heat loss and heat gain.

ENERGY CONSUMPTION

It is the heating and cooling of the house that is the primary and largest consumer of energy. Due to poor construction, inadequate insulation, and other factors, such as inefficient windows, a lot of this energy is wasted. Heat loss to the outside in the winter and heat gain to the inside in the summer increase heating and cooling costs beyond what they would be, were adequate construction and energy-efficient windows used.

A major factor in using energy-efficient windows in addition to lower energy consumption is the comfort of the occupants. For example, if the glazing is cold, as it is with single-glazed windows, our body heat is drawn to the cold window. The interior glass on double-glazed energy-efficient windows is much warmer, so the occupant does not feel the great loss of heat to the window. In the summer the inflow of solar heat gain is reduced, enabling the occupant to be more comfortable at less cost. To accomplish this the selection of windows is important.

Even if the windows and doors are kept closed, the house loses heat in the winter to the outdoors and in the summer gains heat on the inside. This occurs by **conduction**, **infiltration**, **radiation**, and **convection**.

Thermal conduction is a process of heat transfer through a material in which kinetic energy is transmitted

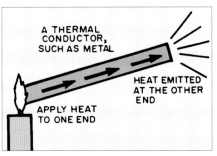

4-2 Heat applied to a material moves through it by conduction.

particle to particle through the material without actual displacement of the particles (4-2). Heat actually travels through walls (an assembly of materials) and glass windows, and through the window frame by conduction (4-3). The greater the difference in temperature between the exterior air and the interior air, the faster the heat will be conducted.

Since glass is a good thermal conductor, it is important to use energy-efficient glazing to reduce heat loss and gain. A single glass panel may have only a few degrees' difference between its outside surface temperature and the inside surface temperature. In cold weather it conducts considerable cold into the room. This greatly increases energy consumption. Multiply the heat loss or gain by the number of single-glazed windows in the house and the energy costs are greatly increased.

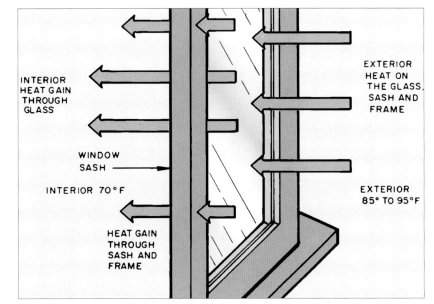

4-3 Heat is transferred through materials by thermal conduction. Glass is a good conductor of heat.

4-4 These energy-efficient vinyl replacement windows greatly reduce heat loss and gain.

Conduction can be controlled by replacing inefficient windows with energy-efficient ones that have double glazing with argon gas between the panes and a frame made of a material that has good insulating values. The frame can make up approximately 20 percent of the area of the window, so selection is important to reduce conduction. Wood and vinyl frames are energy efficient and widely used. Storm windows will create a dead-air space and reduce conduction some. However, a better but more expensive solution is to replace old, inefficient windows with the new energy-efficient replacement windows on the market (4-4). Review Chapter 7 for more information.

Infiltration involves the leakage of air through places such as poorly fitting sash and cracks around the window frame (4-5). Even a very small crack will over a period of hours admit a large volume of air. Old, poorly fitting windows can have infiltration reduced by adding storm windows, weather stripping, and caulking around them on the outside wall. A better but more expensive solution is to install energy-efficient replacement windows or storm windows.

Convection occurs when the air gives up heat to a cooler surface such as a window glass (4-6). The cooled air sinks to the floor, pulling new warmer air against the cold glass, which creates a draft within the room. If a person is seated near a single-glazed window, this draft can be very uncomfortable; you might want to pull the draperies over the window.

Radiation is the transfer of heat as infrared electromagnetic waves through the glass. It moves

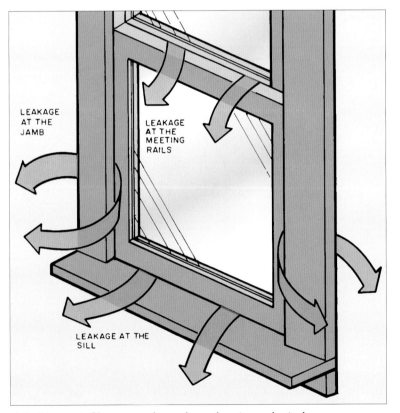

LEAKAGE AT THE JAMB

LEAKAGE AT THE MEETING RAILS

LEAKAGE AT THE SILL

4-5 Air can infiltrate poorly made or deteriorated windows. It does not take long for leakage to allow a large amount of air to enter around the window.

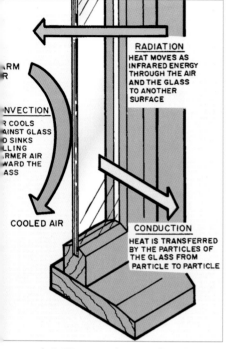

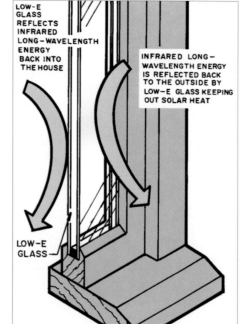

4-6 Heat can be transferred by convection, radiation, and conduction.

4-7 Low-E coatings reflect the long-wavelength radiant heat, providing a means for rejecting unwanted solar heat and helping maintain interior heat.

4-8 Short-wavelength visible light passes through the glass, providing heat to any surface it strikes.

from a warmer source to a cooler one (4-6). As it moves toward the cooler source, it does not heat the air but heats the item it strikes, such as a person. Window glass absorbs heat and radiates it to the other side. If you stand near a burning woodstove, you feel the radiant heat. If you sit near a window, your body radiates heat to the cold glass, making you feel cold.

Only part of the sun's energy is visible. The **shorter wavelengths** beyond purple are ultraviolet (UV), whereas the **longer wavelengths**, those beyond the red part of the visible spectrum of the sun's energy, are infrared and are felt as heat. As the sun strikes the window, heat, ultraviolet wavelengths, and visible light enter the room. Here they may be absorbed and radiated into the room or reflected to other parts of the area.

Long-wavelength radiant heat loss or gain can be overcome somewhat by placing a low-E coating on the glass. This coating reflects the infrared

wavelengths (4-7). Short-wavelength visible light that passes through the glass to the interior will be absorbed by interior surfaces it strikes and the heat gained will be radiated as heat (4-8). This can be reduced if desired by lowering blinds or draperies over the windows when the sun is on them, blocking the visible light. However, this does provide a source of solar heat in the winter as well as natural light.

Solar-control window film is another product that is used to provide solar-heat control and ultraviolet-radiation control. The film is a polyester substrate with a special scratch-resistant coating on one side. It is applied to the interior surface of the glass. It reduces the transmittance of light and infrared heat through glass and has ultraviolet absorbers to reduce the amount of ultraviolet radiation transmitted through the glass. This product is placed on the windows after they are installed.

ENERGY-EFFICIENCY FACTORS

TABLE 4-1 TYPICAL WINDOW PERFORMANCE DATA

Glazing	Center of glass U-factor	Unit U-factor	Center of glass R-value	Unit R-value	% Relative humidity when moisture forms at center of glass	Inside surface glass temp.	Shading coefficient	
Single	1.10	0.85	0.9	1.3	14%	16°F	1.0	
Double	0.25	0.30	4.3	3.1	66%	59°F	0.54*	0.35**
Triple	0.20	0.24	5.8	4.4	74%	61°F	0.50*	0.40**

*High-performance   **High-performance/sun-insulating

WINDOW-RATING FACTORS

The efficiency of windows can be rated by a number of factors determined by testing the units. Factors frequently used include the R-value (resistance to heat transmission), U-factor (heat transmission), Solar Heat Gain Coefficient (SHGC), Visible Light Transmission (VLT), air infiltration, the Condensation Resistance Factor (CRF), and the water-resistance rating.

R-VALUE

The **R-value** is sometimes used to indicate the efficiency of a window. It is a measure of a window's or skylight's ability to **resist** the flow of heat through it. The greater the R-value, the greater the resistance to heat transmission. R is the reciprocal of the U-factor, or R = 1/U. R-value is expressed in units of Btu per hour per square foot of surface area per degree Fahrenheit (F), or watts per square meter per degree Celsius (C) per degree difference between the inside and outside air temperature. Typical window R-value ratings are in **Table 4-1**.

U-FACTOR

The **U-factor** is a measure of the rate of non-solar heat flow through a window or skylight. The smaller the U-factor, the less heat will flow through the unit. It is the reciprocal of total resistance, R. In other words, U = 1/R. It is expressed in units of Btu per hour per square foot of surface per degree Fahrenheit (F), or watts per square meter per degree Celsius (C) per degree difference between the inside and outside air temperature.

The U-factor rating includes the effects of the glazing, the frame, the sash, and on double-glazed units the edge spacer material. The spacer is a compound that separates the two glazing panes, forming an airspace.

Typically the U-factor for an analysis of a total window should be at least 0.5, and something like 0.4 or lower would be strongly recommended. Typical U-factors are in **Table 4-1**.

Solar-heat gain is the heat from solar radiation that will enter a building through a window. It is rated by a Solar Heat Gain Coefficient (SHGC), which is the fraction of available solar heat that will pass through a window. It uses a scale of 0 to 1. A rating of 1 means that 100 percent of the available solar heat passes through, while a rating of 0 means no solar heat passes through. Windows with an SHGC of 0.4 or less are recommended in hot southern and western areas. In the middle and northern states an SHGC of 0.5 would be adequate.

Another way heat gain through glazing is reported is by giving the gain in terms of British thermal units per square foot per hour (Btu/ft²/hr). Examples of typical heat gains for several types of glazing are in **Table 4-2**. Window manufacturers have these data for their products.

Visible Light Transmittance (VLT) rating is the percentage of the visible light spectrum, weighted to the sensitivity of the eye, that will pass through the glazing. The higher the percentage, the more visible light that will pass through. A VLT of 0.6 or higher is recommended for windows where good light transmission is wanted or where good external visibility is required.

Air infiltration includes the leakage due to the glass, sash, and frame. It is measured as a specified pressure difference between the air inside and the air outside the building. Leakage is expressed in cubic feet per minute per square foot of window area or cubic feet per minute per foot of window perimeter. Lower rating numbers indicate a more airtight window. Recommended maximum leakage is 0.34 cubic feet per minute per square foot (cfm/ft²). Lower values are recommended in areas having frequent high levels of wind.

The **Condensation Resistance Factor (CRF)** is a measure used to evaluate a window's resistance to condensation. The rating can be used to ascertain whether the window rated will not have condensation form on the interior surface if the relative humidity of the air in the house is maintained at the recommended level for the part of the country in which the window is to be used. The relative indoor humidity required will vary with the outdoor temperature, which influ-

TABLE 4-2 TYPICAL HEATING GAINS FOR CLEAR GLASS*

Clear glazing	Heat gain*
Single-pane ⅛"	214
Single-pane ³⁄₁₆"	208
Double-pane	186
Double-pane/ high-performance	113

*Btu/ft²/hr

ences the surface temperature of the glass. There is additional information on condensation in Chapter 1.

Thermally efficient windows will be subject to condensation's forming under conditions where the humidity is high either inside or outside the house. The windows are not the cause of the condensation. They prevent interior moisture from escaping to the outside and so are the surface upon which it forms. The CRF will help you select energy-efficient windows that are the least likely to have condensation form. This will vary with the geographic area. The higher the CRF, the less likely condensation will form. In general, the colder the outside temperature and the higher the inside humidity, the higher the CRF rating required. A recommended minimum rating is 35.

The **water-resistance rating** indicates the capacity of the window to resist the penetration of water. The rating is in pounds per square foot (PSF) at which no leakage will occur. While the ratings vary by the type and size of window, typical pressures range from 5.25 to 15 psf (pounds per square foot). A water-resistant window assembly will also have very low air infiltration and therefore be energy efficient.

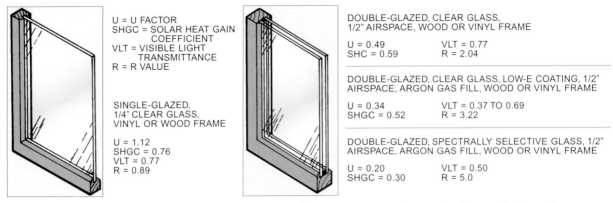

U = U FACTOR
SHGC = SOLAR HEAT GAIN COEFFICIENT
VLT = VISIBLE LIGHT TRANSMITTANCE
R = R VALUE

SINGLE-GLAZED, 1/4" CLEAR GLASS, VINYL OR WOOD FRAME

U = 1.12
SHGC = 0.76
VLT = 0.77
R = 0.89

DOUBLE-GLAZED, CLEAR GLASS, 1/2" AIRSPACE, WOOD OR VINYL FRAME

U = 0.49   VLT = 0.77
SHC = 0.59   R = 2.04

DOUBLE-GLAZED, CLEAR GLASS, LOW-E COATING, 1/2" AIRSPACE, ARGON GAS FILL, WOOD OR VINYL FRAME

U = 0.34   VLT = 0.37 TO 0.69
SHGC = 0.52   R = 3.22

DOUBLE-GLAZED, SPECTRALLY SELECTIVE GLASS, 1/2" AIRSPACE, ARGON GAS FILL, WOOD OR VINYL FRAME

U = 0.20   VLT = 0.50
SHGC = 0.30   R = 5.0

4-9 Typical design values for various assemblies. Manufacturers can provide specific data on their products.

SELECTION OF GLAZING

Energy efficiency is directly influenced by the type of glazing. This relates to the U-factor of the glass and the solar heat gain. A guide to typical values for several types of assembly is in **4-9**. It shows how double glazing greatly reduces the U-factor, solar-heat-gain coefficient, and visible-light transmission. Notice the differences when the glass is not coated and has no argon gas or has a low-E coating or a spectrally selective low-E coating and argon gas. Triple-glazed windows have two dead-air spaces and even better characteristics than those shown. More details are in Chapter 5.

NATIONAL FENESTRATION RATING COUNCIL (NFRC)

The National Fenestration Rating Council is a nonprofit public/private collaboration that provides contractors and home owners with standardized, unbiased methods of comparing various brands and types of window. All NFRC-rated windows are tested using a reliable, standard procedure that measures energy transfer through the entire window unit. U-factors, solar-heat-gain coefficients, visible-light transmittance values, and air-leakage rates are listed on certified windows with the NFRC label (**4-10**). The properties of the windows can be seen by examining the values listed on the label. These are very helpful as you try to choose the right window for the house and its geographic location.

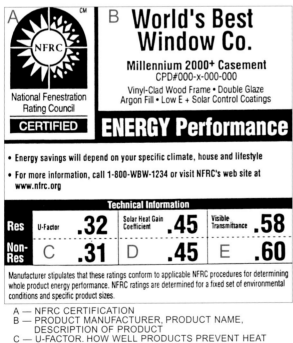

A — NFRC CERTIFICATION
B — PRODUCT MANUFACTURER, PRODUCT NAME, DESCRIPTION OF PRODUCT
C — U-FACTOR. HOW WELL PRODUCTS PREVENT HEAT FROM ESCAPING
D — SOLAR-HEAT-GAIN COEFFICIENT MEASURES HOW WELL PRODUCTS BLOCK HEAT FROM SUNLIGHT
E — VISIBLE TRANSMISSION MEASURES HOW MUCH LIGHT COMES THROUGH THE PRODUCT

4-10 The National Fenestration Rating Council label certifies that the window meets the indicated ratings.

In addition to the large NFRC label on the window, a small permanent NFRC serial code is etched on an inconspicuous part of the window. The large label will be removed when the windows are cleaned after installation, but a future owner can contact NFRC with the serial code to ascertain the brand and rating for the unit.

AMERICAN ARCHITECTURAL MANUFACTURERS ASSOCIATION (AAMA)

Certification has two main purposes: first, to identify the product as meeting the specific standard, and second, to provide a mechanism for a quality-assurance program to assure the consumer that the product conforms and continues to conform to the requirements of the standard. An outside organization not under the control or influence of AAMA is responsible for the validation and administration functions of the program.

The products bearing an AAMA certification label signify that they conform to one of the following product material and performance standards related to windows:

AAMA/NWWDA 101/I.S.2-97 – Voluntary Specifications for Aluminum, Vinyl (PVC), and Wood Windows and Glass Doors

ANSI/AAMA 1002.10-93 – Voluntary Specifications for Insulating Storm Products for Windows and Sliding Glass Doors

NRFC 100-97 – Procedure for Determining Fenestration Product U-factors

Federal Manufactured Housing Construction and Safety Standards:

3280.403 – Primary Windows and Sliding Door

3280.404 – Emergency Exit Windows and Devices

The AAMA certification program provides a thermal testing program by which windows are rated for their thermal and condensation performance. Windows certified carry a certification label (**4-11**). This shows the manufacturer's code number, specification identification, manufacturer's series number, product, grade, class, and the maximum size tested.

The class is designated by a code, such as H-R30, indicating a hung window, residential use with a U-factor of 30.

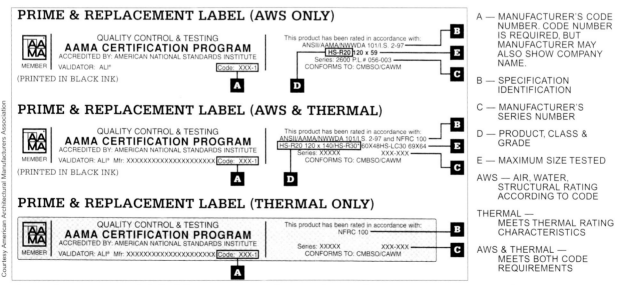

4-11 The certification label of the American Architectural Manufacturers Association. A product carrying this label meets the standards of the specifications indicated on the label.

ENERGY STAR PERFORMANCE RATING

Energy Star Performance requirements for windows and skylights are tailored to fit the energy needs of three climate regions of the country—southern, northern, and central. The Energy Star Climate Region Map label provides a guide for selecting the best windows and skylights for each of these regions. Each region is identified by a color. The northern region is blue, the central is yellow, and the southern is red. Those living in a northern region would look for windows with the label having that region printed in blue. This means the window with this label meets the requirements for energy efficiency for this region. If a window has a label with two or three regions in color, the window can be used in each of the regions (4-12).

The Energy Star program rates the windows using the test data from the National Fenestration Rating Council. This program is discussed in this chapter. Energy Star does not report the test data on its label. The label indicates that the window has qualities needed for the region. This makes it easy for a person who is not familiar with what the actual test results mean to know he or she is selecting the proper window. The performance data for all three regions is in **Table 4-3**.

Windows with the Energy Star label also bear a label from the NFRC that gives the actual test results for energy performance. These include

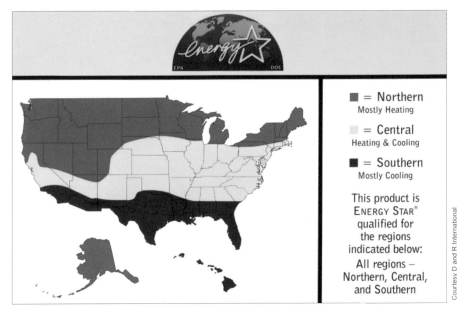

4-12 This Energy Star label indicates the window can be used in all three climate regions.

the U-factor, solar-heat-gain coefficient, and visible transmittance. An NFRC label is shown earlier in **4-10**.

Energy Star windows for the **northern region** include features to reduce heat loss. Windows qualified for the northern climate region must have a U-factor of 0.35 or below. Skylights must have a U-factor of 0.45 or below. Glazing with a low-E coating is a good way to get these ratings.

Windows for the **central region** must have features to reduce both heat loss in the winter and solar heat gain in the summer. Energy Star windows in the region must have a U-factor of 0.40 or below and a SHGC rating of 0.55 or below. Skylights must have a U-factor of 0.45 or below. Low-E coatings on glazing are used to reduce heat loss and heat gain.

Energy Star windows in the **southern region** must include features to reduce solar heat gain. Windows and skylights must have a U-factor of 0.75 or below and a SHGC of 0.40 or below. Low-E coatings and tinted glass help reduce solar heat gain.

TABLE 4-3 PERFORMANCE CRITERIA FOR WINDOWS, DOORS & SKYLIGHTS MEETING ENERGY STAR REQUIREMENTS FOR U.S. NORTHERN, CENTRAL & SOUTHERN REGIONS

ENERGY STAR Climate Region	Windows/Doors U-factor Range (Btu/hr/ft^2/°F)	Windows/Doors SHGC Range	Skylights U-factor Range (Btu/hr/ft^2/°F)	Skylights SHGC Range
Region I (Northern)	0.35 and below	any	0.45 or below	any
Region II (Central)	0.40 and below	0.55 and below	0.50 or below	0.55 and below
Region III (Southern)	0.75 and below	0.40 and below	0.75 or below	0.40 and below

CANADIAN STANDARDS ASSOCIATION (CSA)

The Canadian Standards Association (CSA) sponsors a major publication related to windows. This CSA Standard A440, **Windows**, provides a single set of performance-oriented technical requirements for factory-built windows used in residential and commercial construction, regardless of the material used in the frame and sash members.

The designs are evaluated for airtightness, watertightness, and wind-load resistance. Accompanying this standard are three others. These are *A440.1-98 User Selection Guide to CSA Standard Window A440-98; Windows CSA A440.2-98; Energy Performance of Windows and Other Fenestration Systems and CSA A440.3-98; User Guide to CSA Standard A440.2-98; Energy Performance of Windows and Other Fenestration Systems.*

CSA A440.2-98 is applicable for determining the energy performance properties of a variety of fenestration types including various windows, skylights, sliding glass doors, flat glazings, and curtain walls. It provides the means for determining the **Energy Rating** (**ER**) for fixed and operating windows used in residential housing. It combines the U-value, solar-heat-gain coefficient, and heat losses from air leakage into a single rating so the energy performance of windows can be compared.

The Canadian Standards Association provides certification services for window manufacturers who, under license from CSA, wish to use the appropriate registered CSA marks on certain products to indicate conformity with CSA standards.

CHAPTER 5

Glazing

There has been constant improvement in the glazing materials available. These affect energy efficiency, heat transmittance, visible-light transmittance, ultraviolet light transmittance, sound transmission, fire resistance, and various safety features. The use of multiple layers of glazing, filling the airspace between them with argon or krypton gas, and developing improved edge seals have greatly improved the energy efficiency of window glazing. This reduces heating and cooling costs and ultraviolet damage to furnishings and makes the living space more comfortable. In addition, various coatings and films are used to transmit considerable visible light while reducing heat, ultraviolet radiation, and glare (5-1). All of these technical improvements increase the cost of the window unit. However, over a period of years the savings in energy costs will generally pay for this extra cost and even produce a profit. Increased comfort cannot be given a dollar value but is a very real value produced by energy-efficient glazing.

Courtesy Vista Solar Control (Window film from C.P. Films)

5-1 Window films reduce glare, ultraviolet transmission, and excessive heat gain. Compare with the unprotected glazing seen in 5-3.

GLAZING PROPERTIES

The glazing properties that affect energy performance include the R-value, U-value, heat transmission, solar heat gain, visible-light transmission, air infiltration, and ultraviolet radiation. These are discussed in Chapter 4. As the various types of glazing are considered, these properties are used to compare their performance and energy efficiency. Generalized data for selected glazing materials is in **Table 5-1**.

TABLE 5-1 TYPICAL GLAZING PERFORMANCE DATA*

Material	U-Factor Heat Transmission	R-Value Heat Resistance	Daylight Transmittance Percent
Single clear glass ¼" thick	1.06	0.93	89
Insulating glass ½" airspace	0.52	1.90	80
Glass block 4" thick	0.55	1.80	varies
Insulating glass ¼" thick with low-E film	0.23	4.50	54
Single glass ¼" thick light-green tint	1.13	0.88	75
Single sheet ¼" plastic	0.93	1.08	85
Acrylic block 4" thick	0.49	2.04	varies

*Values will vary slightly for sepcific products.

WINDOW GLASS

There are six basic types of glass. Of these, **soda-lime-silica** is the type most commonly used for door and window glazing. The classification of these materials is based on their ability to resist

TABLE 5-2 THERMAL PROPERTIES OF SEVERAL CATEGORIES OF GLASS

Categories of Glass	Thermal Expansion	Heat Resistance
Soda-lime-silica	High	Low
Lead-alkali-silica	High	Low
Fused silica	Low	High
96% silica	Low	High
Borosilicate (Pyrex)	Medium	Medium
Aluminosilicate	Medium	Medium

heat. Typically the soda-lime-silica glass is composed of 74 percent silica, 15 percent soda, 10 percent lime, and 1 percent alumina. It does not resist high temperatures or rapid temperature changes. When it is struck, it will shatter in small, sharp fragments. A comparison of these six types of glass is in **Table 5-2**.

Glass used in windows—including single-glazed, insulating glass, reflective glass, and tinted glass—is **float glass**. Float glass is produced by a continuous process (5-2). The molten glass is floated across a bath of molten tin. The molten tin gives a very flat surface and supports the ribbon of glass as it is polished by heat from above. This melts out the irregularities. The ribbon of glass moves to the annealing lehr (oven), where the temperature is carefully controlled and is slowly lowered as the glass moves out on rollers, where it is cut to size.

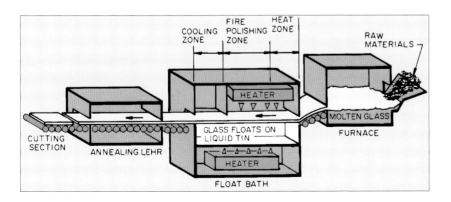

5-2 Float glass is made by a continuous process.

TABLE 5-3 THICKNESSES OF COMMONLY USED FLOAT-GLASS SHEETS

Thicknesses	
inches	mm
3/32	2.5
1/8	3.0
5/32	4.0
3/16	5.0
1/4	6.0
3/8	10.0
1/2	12.0

This process produces sheets of glass that have parallel surfaces, high clarity, and a clear, smooth finish. The process produces **standard annealed glass**. There are three types of float glass. **Silvering glass** is used for high-quality mirrors and optical devices, **mirror glazing** is used for general-purpose mirrors, and **glazing type** is used for door and window glazing.

Float glass is made in a range of thicknesses (**Table 5-3**). The larger the glazed opening, the thicker the glass required.

TEMPERED & HEAT-TREATED GLASS

Tempered glass is used when standard annealed glass is not strong enough. Tempering involves raising the temperature of the glass almost to the softening point and then chilling it by blowing jets of cold air on both sides. Tempered glass is three to five times as resistant to damage as standard annealed glass. If it is broken, it falls in rounded, rather smooth pieces, reducing the danger of serious cuts.

Heat-strengthened glass is heated and cooled as described for tempered glass and is about twice as strong as standard annealed glass.

TINTED GLASS

Glass is tinted by color-producing ingredients that are added to the molten glass in the glass furnace. The color is not a surface coating but is consistent throughout the thickness of the glass. Both glass and plastic glazing can be tinted. The color changes some as the thickness of the glass increases. This affects the solar-heat-gain coefficient, light transmittance, and other properties. These are specified by the manufacturer for each color and thickness of glass.

The tint absorbs some of the natural light and solar heat. In doing so, it reduces glare within the room from brilliant sunlight and reduces the transmission of solar heat.

Tinted glass has adequate transparency from the inside looking out. During the day it provides some privacy when viewed from the outside of the house. At night it is difficult to see outside from the inside and easier to see inside from the outside.

Tinted glass is made to absorb selected parts or all of the solar spectrum and therefore absorb heat. This heat develops within the glass, raising its temperature. A lot of this heat is radiated and convected into the room, so the amount of solar-heat reduction is not as great as other types of glazing. It is much better at reducing glare than at heat reduction.

Tints used are blue-green, bronze, and gray. The **blue-green tint** gives moderate reduction in brightness and glare. The **bronze tint** reduces the transmission of heat. The **gray tint** reduces glare and permits the widest range of natural-light transmission. Other colors are available for special applications. A comparison of properties for typical tinted glass is in **Table 5-4**.

Tinted glazing is durable and used in single- and multiglazed windows. When choosing, check the data on natural-light transmittance and solar-heat gain to get as near the results you want

TABLE 5-4 SOLAR PROPERTIES OF SINGLE-GLAZED TINTED GLASS

Coating	Light (%)		Solar Energy (%)		U-factor Btu/hr/ft^2/°F	
	Transmitted	Reflected	Transmitted	Reflected	Winter	Summer
Sheet clear	91	8	86–89	7	1.13	1.02–1.03
Float clear	79–90	8	58–86	7	1.00–1.13	0.98–1.03
Float blue-green	74–83	7	48–64	6	1.10–1.13	1.08–1.09
Float bronze	26–68	5–6	24–65	6	1.08–1.13	1.08–1.09
Float gray	19–62	4–6	22–63	5	1.06–1.13	1.08–1.09
Float reflective	8–34	6–14	6–37	14–35	0.90–1.11	0.89–1.12

as possible. Remember, it will cut out some heat gain in the summer but also in the winter, when you may want the advantage of solar radiation. Likewise, it reduces light transmission some, which on dark winter days can make the room darker than if clear glazing were used. Since some types of tinted glass will reduce glare and allow light transmission more than they will reduce heat gain, a choice must be made by examining the properties of the available materials.

SPECTRALLY SELECTIVE GLASS

If natural light is important, consider using a spectrally selective glass. It is a coated glazing with optical properties that are transparent to selected wavelengths of energy and reflect shortwave and longwave infrared radiation. One type is a float glass that has specific chemicals added during production. It has a light green or blue tint. Spectrally selective coatings are also used. These are much like those described for sputtered low-E glazing. The number of coatings and their thicknesses affect the reflection of the solar energy.

Spectrally selective coatings filter out 40 to 70 percent of the heat that normally would be transmitted through clear glass, yet allow the full amount of natural light to be transmitted into the house.

Spectrally selective coatings may be applied on tinted glass, producing a glazing product capable of either increasing or decreasing the solar gains to suit the needs of the climate. Since they can reduce air-conditioning costs in warm climates, this reduces the need for electricity in peak seasons.

WINDOW FILM

Window film is an invisible film placed on the window panes. Window film is available as a neutral, nearly invisible coating, and various types provide a range of light transmission. Another type is a reflective film that offers high solar rejection and yet provides excellent visibility from the inside during the day and at night. A low-E film reflects heat back into the house, so it is not absorbed by the glass and conducted to the colder exterior.

Courtesy Vista Solar Control (Window film from C.P. Films)

5-3 Windows before film has been applied can have considerable glare and ultraviolet penetration. Window films reduce glare, ultraviolet transmission, and excessive heat gain. Note the difference in glare between unprotected glazing here and protected glazing after the film has been applied in 5-1.

5-4 Window films are quickly applied to the inside of existing windows by professional installers.

Window films are effective in reducing the transmission of ultraviolet rays, which fade fabrics, carpet, and wallpaper. Some types block over 90 percent of the ultraviolet rays. This also greatly reduces the possibility of skin cancer.

Window films reduce glare (5-3), excessive heat gain, and wasted energy.

Typically they are made with a laminate of polyester and metallic coatings combined with a clear, distortion-free adhesive system and a scratch-resistant face coating—providing a surface with almost total optical clarity.

Window films are professionally applied by a local dealer on the inside of the windows (5-4). The surface can be cleaned with normal window-cleaning products. If the glass is broken, the film holds most of the fragments in place so they do not scatter over the room.

SAFETY FILM

Safety film is applied to glazing to provide some protection when glass shatters. It may have some sun-control properties. Film provides resistance to damage by impact and damage from storm debris. It provides a limited deterrence to vandalism. Remember, it only provides protection for the glazing. The window frame must be such that it withstands damage or forced entry based on its properties. It does reduce visible-light transmittance and slightly obscures the view.

REFLECTIVE GLASS

Reflective glass reduces the amount of solar energy transmitted through the window glass. As the solar energy contacts a glass surface, the energy can be reflected, pass through the glass, or be

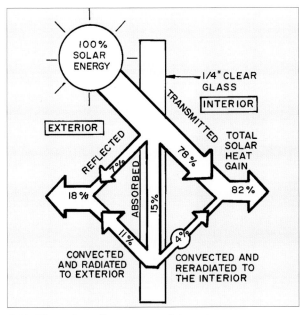

5-5 Clear glass allows most of the solar energy to pass into the room.

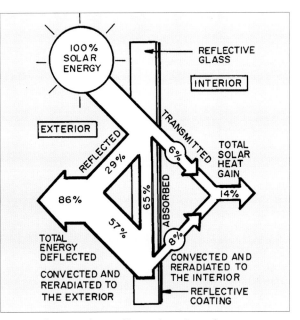

5-6 Reflective glass will greatly reduce the transmission of solar energy into the room.

absorbed. Energy that is absorbed will be partly transmitted into the room and partly radiated back outside. The solar-heat gain of the glass is that part that is transmitted into the room. Notice in **5-5** that 82 percent of the solar energy passes through the clear glass into the room.

Reflective glass blocks the transmission of a high percentage of solar energy, as the example shown in **5-6** illustrates. In this example 86 percent of the solar energy is reflected back to the outside.

Reflective glass has one surface covered with thin, transparent layers of metallic film. Various products produce a range of heat-reflection ratings, and several colors are available. The metallic film is placed on the inside surface of the glass, facing into the building if the window is single-glazed. On double-glazed insu-

lating units the metallic film is placed on the side of the inside glass that faces the exterior of the building (5-7).

Visible-light transmittance is greatly reduced, typically ranging from 10 to 45 percent. Consider this loss as a decision is made to use windows with a reflective coating.

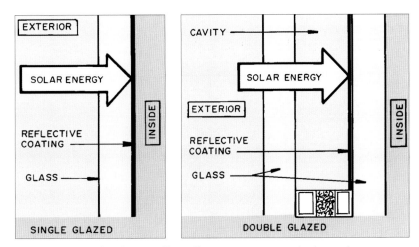

5-7 Locations for the metallic reflective coating on single- and double-glazed windows.

Reflective glazing makes the window appear to those passing by as a mirror (**5-8**). It can produce a lot of heat in the area just outside the window. During the day it acts like a mirror on the outside of the building. During the night it will produce reversed results and reflect the artificial light from lights inside the room back into the room. This can be quite disturbing and difficult on the eyes.

5-8 These reflectively glazed windows mirror the surrounding area.

LOW-E GLAZINGS

Low-E glass (low-emissivity glass) creates a heat barrier that keeps summer heat out and in the winter helps retain heat inside the house. **Emissivity** is the ability of a surface to emit radiant energy. It is used in all climates on single- and multiglazed windows.

Low-E glazing consists of microscopically thin metal or metal-oxide layers on the surface of the window glass. The coating is almost invisible. Typical low-E coatings are transparent to the visible light and shortwave infrared radiation of the solar spectrum, but reflect longwave infrared radiation and emit radiant energy poorly. This suppression of infrared radiation reduces the **U-factor**, which increases the energy efficiency of the glazing. It permits a high level of natural-light transmission. The effect of having a low-E coating on the internal surface of the glazing of a multilayer window unit is to reduce heat transfer across the cavity between the glazings.

Low-E coatings can be applied to either of the interior surfaces of the glass in double-glazed units. The surfaces are numbered as shown in **5-9**. Whether low-E coatings are on surface 2 or 3 affects its performance, because some shortwave solar energy is absorbed by the coatings. Basically, in climates where air cooling is most important the coating is placed on surface 2 (**5-10**). This lowers the solar-heat-gain rating and reduces solar-energy gains. In cold climates where heating is most important, the coating is located on surface 3 (**5-11**). This permits solar energy to pass through the exterior glazing and the cavity, putting the absorbed solar energy on the room-side glass and increasing solar-heat gain in the room.

Low-E coatings may be **hard coat** (pyrolitic) or **soft**

SURFACE 1
EXTERIOR FACE

SURFACE 2
INTERIOR FACE

SURFACE 3
EXTERIOR FACE

SURFACE 4
INTERIOR FACE

EXTERIOR SIDE

INTERIOR SIDE

5-9 The surfaces of the glazing in double-glazed units are identified by a numbering system, counting from the exterior side to the interior side.

coat (sputtered). Generally soft coats have lower emissivities, and so have higher insulation values but do not admit as much solar heat as hard coats. Soft coats are easily damaged and are used only on the interior surfaces of double-glazed units. Hard coats are more durable and can be used on exposed surfaces. While they are thicker than soft coats, they are still very thin.

There are several types of low-E coating and they absorb and transmit different amounts of solar energy. If you live in a northern climate, choose one that admits sufficient solar energy to be useful in the winter, yet blocks some heat gain in the summer.

Heat-transmission low-E coatings are used in northern areas. They permit the transmission of near-infrared solar radiation and reflect the far-infrared radiation (**5-11**). This provides for solar-heat gain in the winter and reduces heat loss from the inside to the exterior.

Selective-transmission low-E coatings are used on window glazing that will be installed in climates where both winter heating and summer cooling requirements are important. In the summer they admit natural light yet reduce solar infrared energy transmission. In the winter they reduce heat loss from the interior of the house. A typical example is shown in **5-10**.

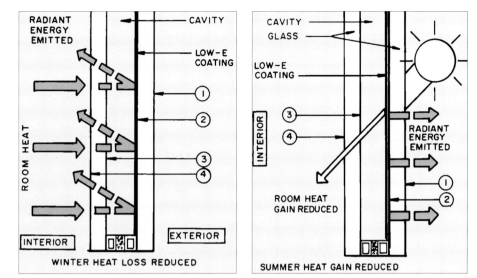

5-10 In areas where air cooling is most important, the low-E coating is placed on the inside of the exterior glass (surface 2) in double-glazed insulating units.

Low-transmission low-E coatings are used in warm climates where the smallest amount of solar-heat gain is desired and the amount of visible-light transmission is best reduced to control glare. Sometimes low-transmission low-E coatings are used on tinted glass as well, to increase the control of heat gain and glare (**5-10**).

The effects of low-E coatings on glazed window units are accounted for in the indicidual ratings for the U-factor, solar-heat-gain coefficient, visible-light transmittance, and ultraviolet transmittance. There is no special single rating for the coating alone.

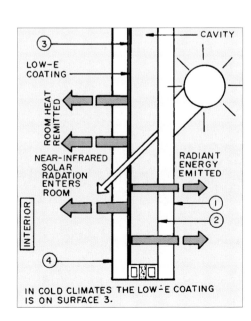

5-11 The low-E coating is placed on the inside face (surface 3) of the interior glass in climates where heating is the major consideration.

INSULATING GLASS

Insulating glass is a glazing unit consisting of two or more layers of glass with an airspace between them. The edges are sealed so the airspace is airtight. The edges of the glass are separated by an edge spacer bonded to the glass. A sealant or glue is used around the perimeter to make the glazing gas- and watertight. The spacer contains a desiccant material that absorbs any traces of moisture left in the airspace after the unit has been sealed. If the spacer is a metal gasket that touches the glass, heat and cold are con-vected through it, reducing the efficiency at the edges of the glazing. To reduce this loss, manu-facturers are using a variety of edge spacers made from materials that have insulating values. One type uses a silicone foam spacer containing a des-iccant. It has adhesive on the edges to seal it to the glass (**5-12**). Another uses a silicone rubber spacer. When metal spacers are used, they are separated from the glass with a sealant or a ther-mal break is placed in the center of the spacer.

The airspace is usually filled with argon or krypton gas. This provides a degree of insulation that reduces the transmission of heat and cold through the glazing.

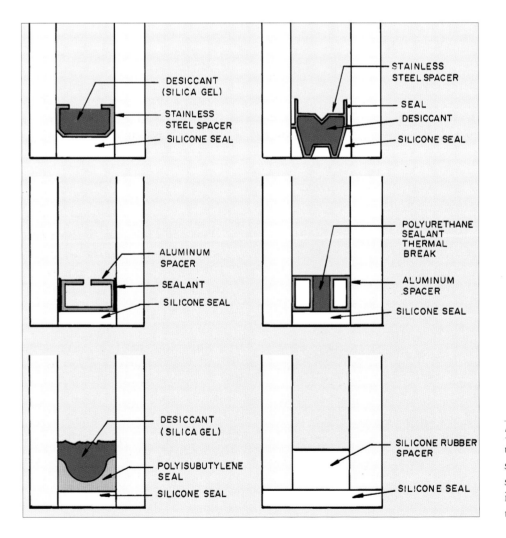

5-12 Insulating glass units have the edges sealed with edge spacers so the cavity is airtight. These are typical spacers in use.

In areas of high wind or unusually high temperatures causing stress on the glass, insulating glass units are made using heat-strengthened or tempered glass. They are available with tinted, reflective, laminated, and low-E glass.

Double-glazed windows are also available with venetian blinds within the airspace (**5-13**). They can be adjusted to reduce glare and block solar radiation; when open or raised, natural light is admitted through the glazing.

These blinds are more effective in reducing energy transfer than the regular interior venetian blinds because only about half of the heat absorbed by the unit is transmitted into the house. They also reduce the U-factor of the window, which reduces the transmission of heat.

These venetian blinds have controls that permit them to be opened, closed, or tilted. They can also be raised and lowered in the same manner as interior venetian blinds.

Units with venetian blinds have an airspace that is not sealed airtight. The airspace can have air seeping into it, so it can develop moisture and possible condensation. To reduce condensation, the airspace is vented to the outside with one or more small tubes.

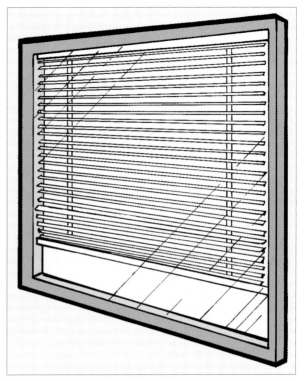

5-13 Narrow venetian blinds can be installed in double-glazed windows, providing protection from glare and blocking solar radiation.

GAS FILLS

The efficiency of multiglazed windows is improved by replacing the air in the cavities with a gas that has a lower conductivity than air. The gases used are inert. **Inert gases** are a group of chemically stable, nonreactive gases that occur naturally in the atmosphere. They are harmless if the window is broken and they are released into the atmosphere.

The most commonly used gas is the inert gas **argon**. It is effective and inexpensive. Another gas used is **krypton**, which is better for reducing heat loss than argon but is more expensive. Krypton is often used in triple- and quadruple-glazed units because, since krypton is more energy efficient than argon, the width of the cavity can be reduced, thus reducing the width of the sash. Typically a ¼-inch-wide cavity is used. Argon-filled glazing cavities are typically ½ inch. The gas does not affect visible-light transmittance.

A well-made, properly sealed multiglazed unit will retain the gas for many years. Some manufacturers use a dual seal around the edge of the unit. A dual seal is more likely to retain the gas in the unit longer than a single seal.

When argon or krypton gas fills the cavities of a multiglazed unit that has low-E coating, the heat transmission by conduction and convection is greatly reduced. This reduces summer heat gain and winter heat loss. Since the interior glass is warmer, condensation is less likely to occur.

POLYVINYL
BUTYRAL
INTERLAYER

5-14 A sample of impact-resistant laminated glass. This product, WinGuard®, has an interlayer of clear polyvinyl butyral, that helps the assembly resist impact from flying debris driven by hurricane-force winds.

5-15 If the blow exceeds the design capabilities of the laminated glass, the fragments will remain bonded to the polyvinyl butyral interlayer.

LAMINATED GLASS

Laminated glass is used in areas where extra protection against breakage is needed. A hurricane-prone area is one place where this glass would help give protection against flying debris. This glass is also frequently used on doors.

Laminated glass consists of layers of float glass bonded with interlayers of plasticized polyvinyl butyral (PVB) resin or polycarbonate (PC) resin. The glass is chemically strengthened by immersing it in a molten salt bath. The example shown in **5-14** provides protection against flying debris and hurricane-force winds. It does not need protection by shutters or plywood panels. Should it be broken, the polyvinyl butyral interlayer keeps the window intact so there is no interior damage (**5-15**). This glazing also reduces noise transfer and ultraviolet radiation into the room. Laminated glass is so strong that it increases security by reducing the chance of its being broken to allow entry into the house. A typical installation in a heavy-duty aluminum frame is shown in **5-16**. The frame used must be strong enough to resist the same damaging forces as the glass.

5-16 This installation of impact-resistant windows and doors uses a strong aluminum frame designed to resist hurricane forces and uses impact-resistant laminated glass.

5-17 This circle-top over an awning window has high-impact glazing.

High-impact laminated glass is available in all types of window including the unit shown in **5-17**. This unit has awning windows crowned by a circle top.

ACOUSTICAL GLASS

Acoustical glass is a form of a laminated glass. It has a layer of sound-absorbing plastic bonded between layers of glass. The soft plastic interlayer permits the glass panels to bend slightly in response to the pressure from the sound waves. It is also available in multipane insulated glazed units.

Two panes separated by an airspace are better than a single pane. The thicker the glass, the better it resists sound transmission. Wider airspaces will have a greater sound-transmission loss. Some use a glass pane and a plastic pane with an airspace. Of course, the window must be tightly sealed. Sound as well as air can filter in around a poorly fitting window. Generally, for residences, the recommended sound level is 30 to 40 dBA (decibel scale).

TABLE 5-5 TYPICAL SOUND TRANSMISSION CLASS (STC) RATINGS

Single Glass Thickness (inches)		STC
⅛		23
¼		28
½		31

Laminated Glass Thickness (inches)		STC
¼		34
⅝		36
½		37
⅝		38

Double-Glazed Dimensions (inches)		
Glass	Airspace	STC
3/32 × 3/32	5/16	31
¼ × 3/16	5/16	31
⅛ × ⅛	½	28

The rating system used for describing the sound-transmission properties for windows is a single number identified as the **Sound Transmission Class (STC)**. In **Table 5-5** are some STC values of several thickness of single glass and paned with an airspace.

GLASS BLOCKS

Glass blocks are available as solid and cavity units made in square and rectangular shapes. The hollow units are made by fusing two halves of pressed glass together. The cavity provides insulating value, giving a typical block a U-factor of about 0.50. They are very strong and provide a secure glazed opening.

Glass blocks are available with a variety of surface patterns and can serve as solar glazing in openings exposed to the sun. The pattern also controls privacy and light transmission (**5-18**). Some provide a great deal of privacy. The patterned surface determines the amount of visual exposure. Other blocks are clear and provide greater exposure. The closer you are to the glass-block window, the more clearly you can see through it. Also keep in mind that at night it is easier to see through from outside when the interior lights are on (**5-19**).

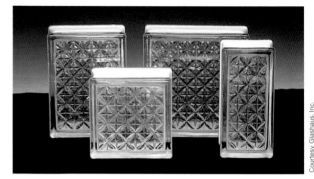

5-18 Glass blocks are available in square and rectangular shapes. Some special shapes, such as curved blocks, are also available.

Glass blocks are fire resistant and can be used in some fire-rated window assemblies. The fire-rating requirements are specified by code, and some glass-block window assemblies will meet requirements for 45-, 60-, or 90-minute window assemblies. To accomplish this the size of the window, type of frame, and type of wall construction must be considered.

Glass blocks available include square and rectangular shapes as well as a variety of units with curved edges or surfaces (**5-20**). Tinted blocks are also available (**5-21**). Typical sizes are 6-, 8-, and 12-inch square with thicknesses of 5¾, 7¾, and 11¾ inches.

Special blocks are made for applications such as turning a corner, ending a row, or forming an installation that curves continuously (**5-22**).

Glass-block windows are available in prefabricated panels. The two-inch-thick blocks weigh up to ⅓ less than conventional glass blocks. They are assembled in an aluminum frame that has integral nailing fins, as used on other types of window. The glass blocks are assembled with a silicone sealant rather than a masonry mortar, making a smooth, attractive assembly (**5-23**).

5-19 These glass blocks provide the privacy that a standard window would not, while allowing sufficient natural light.

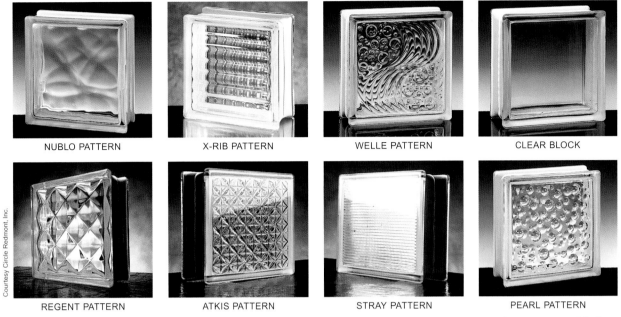

NUBLO PATTERN X-RIB PATTERN WELLE PATTERN CLEAR BLOCK

REGENT PATTERN ATKIS PATTERN STRAY PATTERN PEARL PATTERN

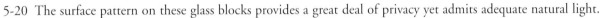

5-20 The surface pattern on these glass blocks provides a great deal of privacy yet admits adequate natural light.

5-21 Glass blocks are available in light color tints.

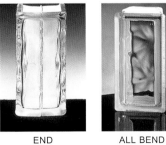

CORNER END ALL BEND

5-22 Glass blocks are available for ending a row, forming a corner, or laying a curved wall.

5-23 Prefabricated glass-block panels use two-inch-thick blocks. Each weighs 3.6 pounds or 1.8 pounds less than a conventional glass block. This 48 x 48-inch panel weighs about 150 pounds.

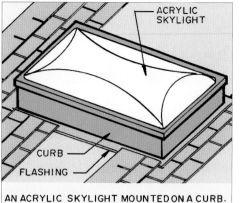

AN ACRYLIC SKYLIGHT MOUNTED ON A CURB.

ACRYLIC SKYLIGHT

CURB

FLASHING

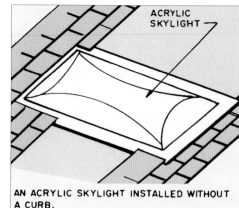

ACRYLIC SKYLIGHT

AN ACRYLIC SKYLIGHT INSTALLED WITHOUT A CURB.

5-24 Some low-profile skylights are molded from acrylic plastic.

PLASTIC GLAZING

Plastic glazing materials are available in sheet form for windows and molded form for skylights (5-24). They are lightweight and easy to use. Since they are not as brittle as glass, they do not shatter in sharp shards and are actually quite tough.

When exposed to fire, plastic glazing will melt and burn, producing noxious fumes, so it is not used in any place where fire resistance is a factor. Some types of plastic glazing screen out most of the ultraviolet radiation. Plastic glazing has a higher rate of thermal expansion than glass and will not function as well as glass in environments of high or low temperatures. It is not generally used in insulated multiglazed window units. Over a period of time plastic glazing will degrade due to exposure to sun and the weather.

CLEAR PLASTIC GLAZING

There are a number of plastic glazing materials in use. Probably the most commonly used type is a **clear acrylic**. It has an impact strength 10 to 15 times that of various types of window glass and has a light transmission of around 90 percent. It is available in several tints. It is soft, so be careful when you clean it or it will become heavily scratched. Do not use abrasive cleaners. Rinse with water and wipe with a soft cloth. A **frosted** acrylic is often used in skylights because it diffuses the incoming light. If used on windows, the view is obstructed.

Clear polycarbonate sheets are also used for glazing. While more expensive than acrylic, they have an impact strength up to 30 times that of acrylic and 250 times that of glass. Polycarbonate glazing is suitable in areas where high security is needed, and it is used to produce bullet-resistant panels. Light transmission varies with the thickness, but a 0.125-inch sheet has a rating of 86 percent.

ACRYLIC BLOCKS

Another plastic glazing material is **acrylic blocks**. They appear much the same as glass blocks but are considerably lighter than glass blocks (5-25). Since they are lightweight, they are used in fixed and operable windows such as casement and awning types.

These blocks are a scratch-resistant high-quality acrylic that will stand up against harsh weather conditions and resist discoloration. They are available with several surface patterns, a frosted finish, and a clear surface.

Acrylic blocks are made by hermetically sealing two cast pieces, creating a cavity that provides an insulating airspace. The U-factor is about the same as that of the typical dual-glazed window.

5-25 Acrylic blocks can be used to glaze large and small wall openings and control light and heat transfer.

Courtesy Hy-Lite Products, Inc.

Acrylic blocks are available in 6-inch and 8-inch squares, rectangular shapes, and diamond blocks in 2-inch and 3-inch thicknesses. Several tints are also available (**5-26**).

Manufacturers offer acrylic blocks mounted in frames forming a ready-to-install window unit (**5-27**). Aluminum and vinyl frames are available in several colors.

Acrylic blocks can be cleaned with a mild liquid soap and lukewarm water. The surface of the blocks should be wiped with a soft cloth once the surface is free of grit. If the blocks have dirt on them, direct water to the surface to soften the dirt first and then wash dirt away with water pressure from a garden hose. Never use an abrasive cleaner or directly wipe off grit.

Courtesy Hy-Lite Products, Inc.

5-26 Acrylic blocks are available in several shapes. This is a diamond-block casement window.

Courtesy Hy-Lite Products, Inc.

5-27 This is a preassembled acrylic block window unit that is installed in much the same way as conventional windows.

SUPER-WINDOWS

A super-window is a highly insulated window that has a winter heat loss lower than that of the typical insulated exterior wall into which it is installed. The amount of heat that the window admits under winter sunlight conditions is **greater than its total heat loss** when added up over a 24-hour period. Therefore in cold climates the window actually provides more heat to the interior than it loses to the cold exterior. The development of these windows focuses on improved, energy-efficient sash, frames, and edge seals on the multipane glazing. Units being developed have insulating values several times higher than those of typical double-glazed windows. The average performance should approach an R-5 value.

Typical super-windows available are triple- or quadruple-glazed units with two low-E coatings, improved low-conductance spacers, energy-efficient sash and frames, and krypton or argon gas fill. The center glazing may be plastic or glass panes (**5-28**). Optical properties such as solar transmittance can be designed specifically for various climate zones.

ALTITUDE CONSIDERATIONS

Manufacturers have their window units tested for use in various altitudes. Using double-pane insulating glass at altitudes higher than its rating will result in glass distortion and increased possibility of breakage. As the altitude increases, the atmospheric pressure decreases, causing the sealed glazing to expand its volume to reduce the interior pressure. This causes the glass to deflect, which when large can cause damage. The difference in pressure is also applied along the edge seal, resulting in seal failure.

Some window manufacturers have developed glass technology that increases altitude limits on energy-efficient glazed units to as high as 10,000 feet. When selecting windows in various locations that have possible altitude problems, check with the manufacturer to verify the suitability of the windows chosen. For example, Andersen Windows, Inc., has data on windows for altitudes from 3,000 to 10,000 feet.

WIND LOAD

Building codes require exterior windows to withstand specified design wind loads. The requirements will vary depending upon the geographic

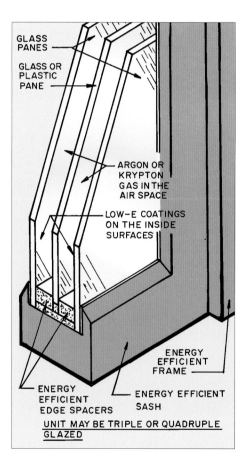

GLASS PANES

GLASS OR PLASTIC PANE

ARGON OR KRYPTON GAS IN THE AIR SPACE

LOW-E COATINGS ON THE INSIDE SURFACES

ENERGY EFFICIENT FRAME

ENERGY EFFICIENT EDGE SPACERS

ENERGY EFFICIENT SASH

UNIT MAY BE TRIPLE OR QUADRUPLE GLAZED

5-28 Super-window design permits the winter sun to introduce more heat into the house than is lost. Details vary depending upon the manufacturer.

location. Areas where high winds can be expected, such as coastal areas that are subject to hurricanes, will have higher design loads. Performance requirements consider the typical basic wind speed and the height and exposure of the area. Exposure refers to the location, such as a large city, suburban area, open terrain with obstructions such as trees and undulation in typography, and open, flat, unobstructed areas. The height is considered because wind speed increases with the height above the ground.

Some window manufacturers provide design data specifying the design wind load on their various windows, including special situations such as a row of windows or vertical stacks. The length of the mullion is considered as the data is presented.

BUILDING CODES

Building codes prescribe the performance and construction requirements for **exterior window systems** installed in wall systems. Typical areas where performance standards are specified are listed in **Table 5-6.** Consult the local code for specific data.

TABLE 5-6   TYPICAL BUILDING CODE PERFORMANCE SPECIFICATION AREAS FOR EXTERIOR WINDOW SYSTEMS

SHEET-GLAZED WINDOWS

Resistence to wind loads	The specific data vary by geographic location. Areas along the coast will have higher requirements.
Testing and labeling	Window units must be by an approved independent laboratory. Label must identify the manufacturer, the inspection agency, and performance characteristics.
Hurricane-prone areas	Requires windows meeting windborne-debris specifications.
Window unit installation	Must be anchored to the main force-resisting system of the building as per code specifications.
Mullion specification	Mullions between individual window assemblies must be tested by an approved testing laboratory and meet code performance criteria.

GLASS-BLOCK PANELS

Hollow glass-block units	Minimum thickness of the glass face specified.
Standard glass blocks & thin glass blocks	Total thickness of the block is specified.
Exterior panels	Assembled glass-block panel must meet standards for exterior standard-unit and exterior thin-unit panels. Separate specifications are given for interior and curved panels.
Panel support	Glass-block panel support is specified giving deflection, lateral-support, and panel-anchor restraints.

Sill protection for glass-block installations
Requirements for providing **expansion joints**.
Type of **mortar** used on mortar-laid glass block.
Proper **reinforcement** of horizontal joints when the blocks are laid in mortar.
Placement of glass blocks, including thickness of head and bed joints.

Installing Windows in New Construction

The installation of windows is quite an important part of finishing the exterior of a house. They are expected to operate easily and completely block penetration by water and air. The exact method of installation will vary somewhat depending upon the manufacturer of the window. Each company has developed its units to provide the best service possible and be easy to install. In this chapter are presented a series of general techniques that are relatively common to all brands. Before installing any window consult the installation manuals and view the installation videos the manufacturer can provide.

After the windows arrive on the site, they should be stored in a dry location and placed upright. Never lay them flat or on the side jambs. Do not stack more than 3 or 4 windows against each other. Since they are heavy, get someone to help carry them to the storage area. Do not drag or push them along the ground or subfloor. The storage area should be cool and dry. Excess heat or direct hot sunlight can cause vinyl units to warp.

THE ROUGH OPENING

The framing carpenters will have prepared the rough opening (**6-1**). The window manufacturer will specify the required rough-opening dimensions. Typically the rough-opening width will be ½ inch (12mm) wider than the frame and the height ½ inch (12mm) to ¾ inch (18mm) larger. Measure the size of the rough opening at each side and in the center as shown in **6-2**. The smallest

6-1 This is a typical framed rough window opening. It must be sized carefully, following the manufacturer's directions.

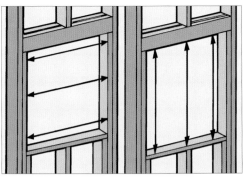

6-2 Before installing a window check the size of the rough opening in three places on width and length. The smallest distance should be the same or a little larger than the minimum recommended by the manufacturer.

6-3 Measure the diagonals of the rough opening. These should be equal; if they are not the same, the opening is not square.

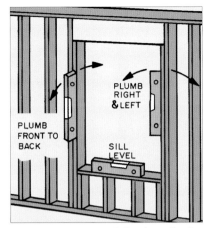

6-4 Use a carpenter's level to check the sides of the rough opening to see whether they are level and plumb.

distance should be the actual rough-opening size. Do not try to force a window into a rough opening that does not have the recommended size.

Next, check the rough opening to see whether it is square. To do this, measure the diagonals. Generally, if they are within ⅛ inch (3mm) of each other, the opening is satisfactory (**6-3**).

Finally, check the framing to see whether it is plumb (**6-4**). If it is out of plumb side to side, the opening will not be square. If it is out of plumb front to back, water may remain trapped in the sill. If set plumb, the water in the sill will drain.

FLASHING TECHNIQUES

There are several ways builders flash the edges of a window to provide protection against moisture and air infiltration. The flashing material used should provide at least four hours of protection against water

penetration. The following examples are for windows secured with fins to the framing of the rough opening. Solid vinyl windows and wood windows clad with vinyl or aluminum typically have mounting fins.

First, prepare the edges of the rough opening. If the sheathing is covered with housewrap (**6-5**), it is cut and lapped over the sides of the rough opening. This is often the only wrap used in

6-5 This exterior wall is covered with housewrap that is folded over the sides of the rough opening and stapled inside as seen in 6-1.

6-7 The plastic flashing material is secured to the outside sheathing and inside framing with nails having large plastic heads.

6-6 This rough opening has been sealed with a plastic flashing material over the housewrap.

6-8 This is how an installation looks from the inside of the house after the window has been installed.

6-9 This vinyl window has been installed over the window flashing.

6-10 In mild climates some installers seal the nailing fin to the housewrap with an adhesive-backed, window-wrap jamb tape.

6-11 The flashing is installed below the sill first and then it is overlapped with the jamb tape. A couple of galvanized nails help secure the overlap.

mild climates. A better technique is to cover the lapped housewrap with a plastic flashing material or builder's paper (**6-6**, 6-7, and **6-8**).

The window is installed by laying a bead of caulking around the rough opening about ¼ inch (6mm) from the edge. Set the window in the caulking and install as recommended by the manufacturer (**6-9**). Finish the flashing by bonding a wide adhesive-backed, window-wrap jamb tape over the fin, sealing it to the housewrap (**6-10** and **6-11**).

A better flashing system is shown in **6-12**. This is especially important in areas having a lot of rain, snow, and winds. Install a strip of building paper at the bottom of the window opening.

Then caulk around the edge of the opening and install the window as directed by the manufacturer. Next, install strips of building paper on the fins on each side. Some builders lay a bead of caulking on the fin and press the paper into it. At the head cut the housewrap about 6 inches (150mm) above the top of the window and install a strip of building paper up under the housewrap and down over the fin. Then tape the slit with housewrap tape, sealing the flashing and housewrap together.

Notice that by following the steps in **6-12**, the side flashing overlaps the bottom flashing and the top flashing overlaps the side flashing and is, in turn, overlapped by the housewrap.

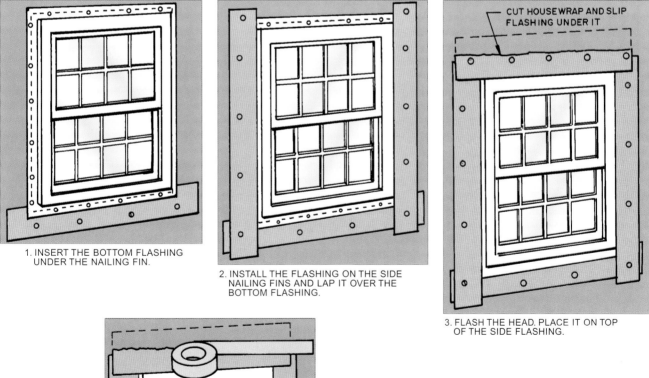

1. INSERT THE BOTTOM FLASHING UNDER THE NAILING FIN.

2. INSTALL THE FLASHING ON THE SIDE NAILING FINS AND LAP IT OVER THE BOTTOM FLASHING.

CUT HOUSE WRAP AND SLIP FLASHING UNDER IT

3. FLASH THE HEAD. PLACE IT ON TOP OF THE SIDE FLASHING.

4. COVER THE SEAM WITH TAPE.

6-12 It is better to flash the nailing fin with wide strips of building paper, starting by inserting the first layer under the sill-nailing fin. These steps reduce the chances for leaks to develop around the window as the house gets older.

A slightly different, but widely used, approach to flashing the nailing fin is shown in **6-13**. After the sides of the rough opening are covered with housewrap, the flashing is installed with the side pieces overlapping the bottom piece. A bead of caulking is laid around the edge of the rough opening and the window is installed on top of the flashing. Then the housewrap is cut above the window and the top flashing is slid under it and over the top fin, as was done in the previous method. The housewrap and flashing are then sealed with window-wrap jamb tape.

If the sheathing is to be covered with asphalt-impregnated building paper, first cover the edges of the rough opening with a 9- or 10-inch-wide strip of building paper. Refer to **6-7**. Install a strip of flashing along the sill of the rough opening (**6-14**). Nail along the top edge of the building-paper strip. The first row of building paper will be slipped up under it. Next, install the window as directed by the manufacturer. Lay a bead of sealer on the nailing flanges before the window is set in place. Now lay a bead of sealer on the nailing fin and install the flashing on the jamb and head. Notice that the head flashing goes over the jamb flashing. The jamb flashing goes over the sill flashing. Now the sheathing can be covered with builder's felt. It should go over the flashing on the jamb and head and under the flashing at the sill.

Unclad solid-wood windows are mounted to the rough-opening framing by nailing through a large wood molding, called brick molding, mounted on the front of the frame. The rough opening is covered with housewrap or building paper. The window is installed as required by the manufacturer. Then an aluminum flashing strip is placed over the molding at the head (**6-15**). The housewrap or building felt is then placed over this flashing and sealed with caulking.

Other flashing situations arise when installing windows such as circle tops, awnings, bows, and bays. The end result should be a watertight, fully sealed flashing that will repel any water that may eventually penetrate the exterior siding material.

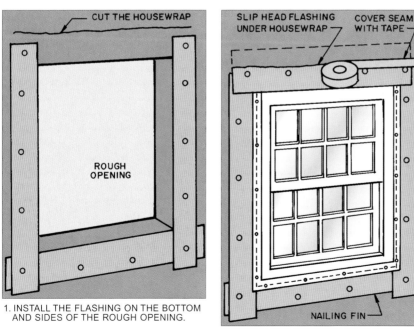

1. INSTALL THE FLASHING ON THE BOTTOM AND SIDES OF THE ROUGH OPENING.

2. INSTALL THE WINDOW AND FLASH THE HEAD.

6-13 This flashing system places building paper around the jambs and sill before the window is installed and over the head nailing fin after the window has been installed.

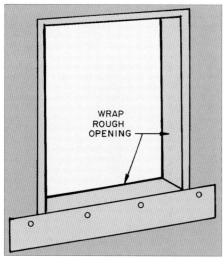

1. INSTALL THE SILL FLASHING. NAIL ON THE TOP EDGE. THE FIRST ROW OF BUILDING PAPER SLIPS UNDER IT.

2. CAULK THE FLASHING AT THE SILL AND INSTALL THE WINDOW.

3. PUT CAULKING ON THE JAMB AND HEAD NAILING FINS AND INSTALL THE FLASHING OVER THEM.

6-14 (Above and right) This is how to flash the rough opening when the exterior sheathing is to be covered with building paper.

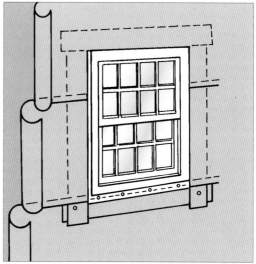

4. INSTALL THE FIRST ROW OF BUILDING PAPER UNDER THE SILL FLASHING. LAY THE ADDITIONAL ROWS OVER THE JAMB AND HEAD FLASHING.

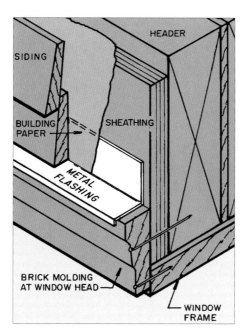

6-15 (Left) Windows installed having a brick molding require that a metal flashing be placed over the molding at the head.

6-16 Many window units are secured to the framing of the rough opening by a nailing fin that is manufactured as part of the unit.

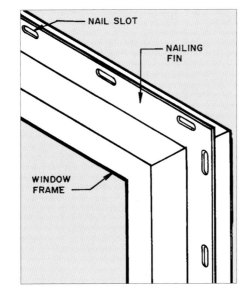

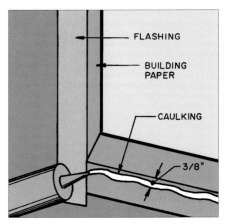

6-17 After the rough opening has been flashed, lay a bead caulking along the edge before placing the window against the framing.

Courtesy Andersen Windows, Inc.

6-18 The window is lifted into the opening and positioned for nailing. It requires more than one person to lift, hold, level, plumb, and nail it properly.

Courtesy Weather Shield Windows & Doors

6-19 Small windows can be set by one person outside and one inside to steady and help level and plumb the window.

INSTALLING WINDOWS WITH NAILING FINS

Most windows used today are either solid vinyl or wood that is vinyl- or aluminum-clad. These are made with a nailing fin that is secured to the sides of the rough opening (**6-16**).

Prepare the opening as described earlier in this chapter. In addition to framing the rough opening, this includes covering the sheathing with building paper or housewrap as well as flashing the edges of the opening using one of the various techniques described earlier, such as overlapping with plastic flashing or building paper.

Now lay a bead of caulking around the perimeter of the rough opening. Keep it about ¼ to ⅜ inch (6 to 10mm) from the edge (**6-17**). Lift the window into the opening (**6-18**). This usually requires two people to lift and hold it in place. Smaller windows will require one person outside to set it in place and one inside to help hold and center it (**6-19**). A very large window requires two or more people to hold it in place while an additional person begins to nail it to the rough-opening framing and check it for levelness and plumb (**6-20**). Heavy windows and those well above the ground require the use of scaffolding as shown in **6-20**.

6-20 Large windows and those some distance above the ground require several persons and a secure work platform.

Courtesy Weather Shield Windows & Doors

WINDOW UNIT
INSTALLATION STEPS

1. Center the window in the rough opening and let it rest on the rough sill. Place shims below each side jamb (**6-21**) and tighten until the window is level (**6-22**).

2. Place a nail in one corner of the nailing fin. Recheck for levelness and place a nail in the other top corner.

3. Now check the jambs for straightness and plumb (**6-23**). Adjust the shims on the jamb until the window is plumb. Now see whether the sash moves easily. If it does, close the sash and lock it.

6-22 After the window is set and shimmed, check to see it is level. Only push the shims by hand; hammering them may warp the frame.

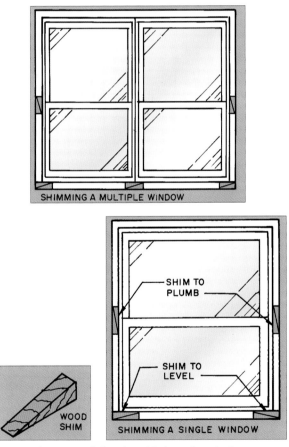

6-23 Check the jambs to be certain they are plumb. Adjust the shims as necessary.

6-21 Shims carefully placed below the window on the sill and along the jambs help hold the unit level and plumb.

6-24 After the window checks level and plumb, measure the diagonals to see whether it is still square. If it is not, the sash will not operate properly.

WINDOWS & SKYLIGHTS

4. Measure the diagonals to be certain the window is square (**6-24**). If one is longer, push on the shims to square up the window frame. Do not hammer the shims. This could cause them to bow the frame and the window will not open properly.

5. Open and close the sash to be certain it is operating smoothly.

When you are working with hung windows, lower the sash to the sill and check to be certain the gap at the sill is the same all across the window (**6-25**). With casement windows check the gap along the open side by the frame. Use the shims to adjust the frame until it is level, plumb, and square.

6. Now install the specified type of nail in the center of the slot or star opening in the upper-right corner (**6-26**).

Use the nail recommended by the manufacturer. Typically these are 1¾-inch galvanized roofing nails or aluminum or stainless-steel nails. The nail should be long enough to penetrate 1 inch (25mm) into the studs that form the rough opening. If the window is properly situated, nail the upper-left corner and place nails in the center of the slots or stars on the fin. These are usually about 6 to 8 inches (152 to 203mm) apart. Do not nail the top fin unless this is recommended by the window manufacturer.

7. Drive the nails snug against the fin but do not hammer them completely tight. This allows a bit of slack to let the frame expand and contract due to temperature changes (**6-27**).

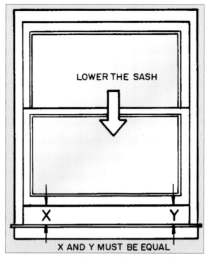

6-25 Check the installation of hung windows by lowering the sash near the sill and measuring the distance between them on each side.

6-26 Begin by placing a nail in the upper-right corner. Set it against the nailing fin but do not hammer it tight against the fin.

6-27 This nailing fin has been secured to the rough-opening framing with galvanized roofing nails.

INSTALLING WINDOWS IN NEW CONSTRUCTION

When installing windows with nailing fins over foam-board sheathing, use special collar-head nails as shown in **6-28**. They must be driven carefully, so when they are snug the foam board has not been crushed.

Some prefer to install a wood trim around a vinyl window as shown in **6-29**. If wood or vinyl siding is to be used, it is advisable to flash it at the head as shown in **6-30**. If vinyl siding is used, the wood trim can be topped with a plastic J-channel that diverts water (**6-31**). J-channels can also be used with vinyl siding if no trim board is used (**6-32**). J-channels form effective water diversion on all sides of the window.

Vinyl-clad wood windows with a fin can have wood or vinyl siding installed as shown in **6-33**. Notice the use of a backer rod and caulking between the window and the siding.

6-28 Large collar-head nails are used when installing the nailing fin over foam-board sheathing. This spreads out the pressure and reduces the chance of crushing the foam board.

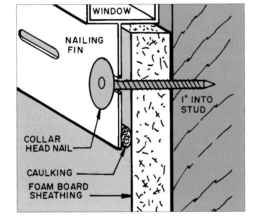

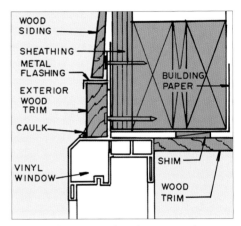

6-30 When a window has a wood trim, it is recommended that the head be protected with metal flashing.

6-29 These vinyl windows have wood trim around the perimeter serving as an architectural feature.

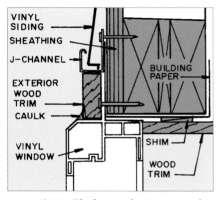

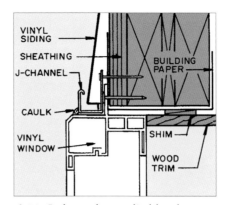

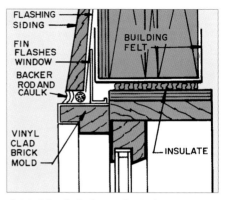

6-31 Flash wood trim around a vinyl window with a J-channel supplied by the manufacturer, if vinyl siding is used.

6-32 J-channels supplied by the manufacturer can also be used to flash the head of vinyl windows even when wood trim is not used.

6-33 Vinyl-clad wood windows with a nailing fin can have wood clapboards or vinyl siding installed over the fin.

INSTALLING UNCLAD SOLID-WOOD WINDOWS

Unclad solid-wood windows are secured to the rough-opening framing by nailing through the brick molding. The window in **6-34** has a wide molding mounted around the front edge. This is typically called a brick molding. The window is mounted as described for vinyl windows. However, it is nailed to the rough-opening fram-ing through the brick molding. Apply a layer of caulking around the edge of the rough opening, set the unit in, plumb, level, and center it, and nail through the brick molding (**6-35**). Use a galvanized finishing nail long enough to go into the wall studs one inch. Set the nail and cover with caulking. Caulk around the edges along the sheathing. Flash the rough opening using one of the various techniques that are described earlier in this chapter.

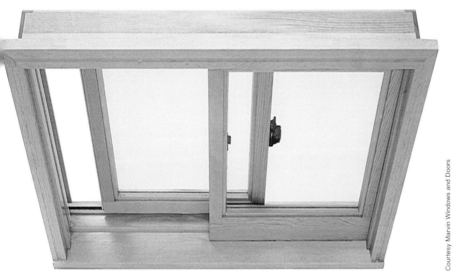

6-34 This unclad solid-wood window has a wide brick molding mounted on the front edge of the frame.

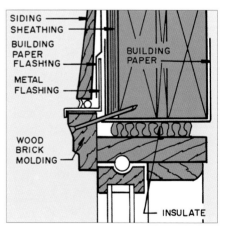

Courtesy Marvin Windows and Doors

6-35 The solid-wood window is secured to the rough-opening framing by nailing through the brick molding. Notice the metal flashing sealing the head.

6-36 Siding is placed close to the brick molding and the space between is sealed with caulking.

6-37 This window has a special base panel installed over the sheathing. The panel is the base upon which coats of synthetic plaster are troweled. The space at the window is then caulked.

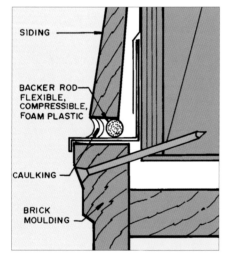

6-38 A backer rod is used to set the depth of the caulking and to provide a firm backing as it is laid into the opening.

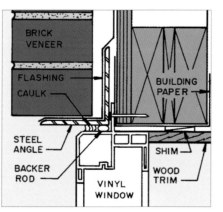

6-39 When vinyl windows are installed in a brick-veneer wall, the flashing is laid over the steel angle that carries the bricks across the window opening.

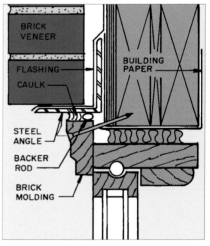

6-40 Unclad windows in a brick-veneer wall are nailed to the rough-opening frame and a steel angle is used to carry the brick across the window opening.

OTHER INSTALLATION DETAILS

After the window has been installed and flashed, the exterior siding can be installed. Place the siding next to the window but leave a small space for caulking. This is especially important when using vinyl siding, because it expands a great deal. Leave at least a ¼-inch (6mm) gap between the window frame and the siding (**6-36**). Another type of siding installation is shown in **6-37**. This sheathing is a special extruded polystyrene insulation panel that is the base for several finishing coats of synthetic plaster. This finish is called an **exterior insulation and finish system** (EIFS).

When installing the caulking, it is recommended that a backer rod be installed. A backer rod is a flexible, compressible rod made of foam plastic (**6-38**). It is placed in the joint to limit the depth the caulking enters the joint and provides a backing so a solid layer of caulking can be installed.

6-41 These vinyl-clad wood windows are in a brick-veneer wall. They are installed in the same manner as described for vinyl windows.

WINDOWS IN MASONRY-VENEER WALLS

Typical installation of a vinyl window in a rough opening when the exterior wall material is brick is shown in **6-39**. The rough opening is flashed as described for windows in walls with wood or vinyl siding and the window is installed as described earlier. The mason lays the bricks up from the foundation around the window. A steel angle is laid at the head to carry the bricks over the width of the window. The space between the bricks and the window frame is caulked. A typical detail for a wood window is shown in **6-40**.

In **6-41** are vinyl-clad wood windows. The brick veneer gives the windows a pleasant recessed appearance. A brick sill is clearly shown in **6-42**. It is sloped to drain water away from the window. Decorative-brick framing details as shown in **6-43** provide another way to add some architectural detail.

6-42 Notice the sloped brick sill below the windowsill. This provides drainage for all the water that may run down the window.

6-43 This vinyl window has a decorative brick framing corbeled around it, providing an interesting architectural feature. Notice the keystone at the center of the arch above the window.

6-44 These acrylic-block windows are cased on the inside of the house in the same manner as other types of window.

Courtesy Hy-Lite Products, Inc.

Courtesy Hy-Lite Products, Inc.

6-45 This is a preassembled window using acrylic blocks in a vinyl or aluminum frame.

Courtesy Hy-Lite Products, Inc.

6-46 Since acrylic blocks are very lightweight, they can be used in the sash of operating windows, as shown in this casement window.

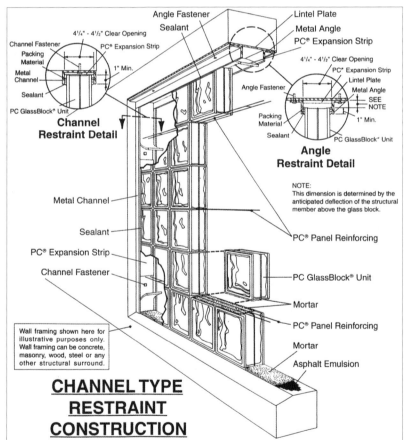

Angle Fastener
Sealant
4¼" - 4½" Clear Opening
PC® Expansion Strip
Channel Fastener
Packing Material
Metal Channel
1" Min.
Sealant
PC GlassBlock® Unit

Channel Restraint Detail

Lintel Plate
Metal Angle
PC® Expansion Strip
4¼" - 4½" Clear Opening
PC® Expansion Strip
Lintel Plate
Angle Fastener
Metal Angle
SEE NOTE
Packing Material
1" Min.
Sealant
PC GlassBlock® Unit

Angle Restraint Detail

NOTE:
This dimension is determined by the anticipated deflection of the structural member above the glass block.

Metal Channel
Sealant
PC® Expansion Strip
Channel Fastener

PC® Panel Reinforcing
PC GlassBlock® Unit
Mortar
PC® Panel Reinforcing
Mortar
Asphalt Emulsion

Wall framing shown here for illustrative purposes only. Wall framing can be concrete, masonry, wood, steel or any other structural surround.

CHANNEL TYPE RESTRAINT CONSTRUCTION

Courtesy Pittsburgh Corning Corporation

6-47 This shows the installation details for a glass-block window using cement mortar between the rows of blocks. It uses a metal channel mounted on the head and jamb of the rough opening.

INSTALLING ACRYLIC-BLOCK WINDOWS

Acrylic-block windows are installed in the same manner described earlier for other windows. The rough opening is flashed, a bead of caulking is laid around the edge, and the window is inserted in the opening, checked for level and plumb, and secured to the framing for nailing through the fin with roofing nails. On the interior the window is cased as desired (**6-44**). Acrylic-block windows are available preassembled with aluminum and vinyl frames. The assembled unit has a nailing fin as described earlier in this chapter for other types of window (**6-45**).

Acrylic-block sash are very light in weight and are used to glaze operating windows. The casement window shown in **6-46** gives the desired privacy yet can be opened to provide ventilation.

INSTALLING GLASS-BLOCK WINDOWS

Glass blocks have been installed for years using mortar joints to bond them together in a manner similar to bricks. This produces a strong, fire-resistant window installation. More recently a number of other systems have been developed making the installation easier.

INSTALLING GLASS BLOCK USING MORTAR JOINTS

A mortar installation that uses a metal channel installed on the sides and top of the rough opening is shown in **6-47**. The installation can be made without the channel, and the glass blocks butt an expansion strip and a panel anchor mounted on the sides of the opening (**6-48**). A finished installation is shown in **6-49**.

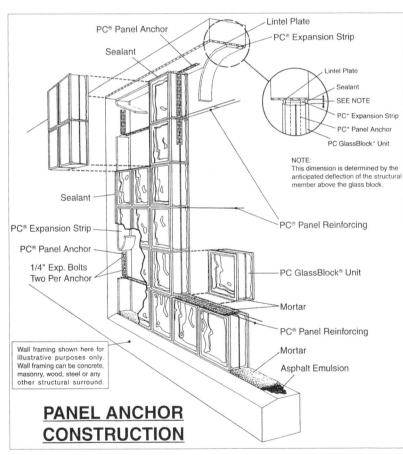

PANEL ANCHOR CONSTRUCTION

PC® Panel Anchor
Sealant
Lintel Plate
PC® Expansion Strip
Lintel Plate
Sealant
SEE NOTE
PC® Expansion Strip
PC® Panel Anchor
PC GlassBlock® Unit

NOTE:
This dimension is determined by the anticipated deflection of the structural member above the glass block.

Sealant
PC® Expansion Strip
PC® Panel Anchor
1/4" Exp. Bolts Two Per Anchor
PC® Panel Reinforcing
PC GlassBlock® Unit
Mortar
PC® Panel Reinforcing
Mortar
Asphalt Emulsion

Wall framing shown here for illustrative purposes only. Wall framing can be concrete, masonry, wood, steel or any other structural surround.

Courtesy Pittsburgh Corning Corporation

6-48 This method for installing glass blocks with mortar uses panel anchors on each row and an expansion strip on the head and jamb.

6-49 This glass-block installation was made in a wall using brick veneer. The blocks are secured to the rough-opening framing and the brick carried over the window opening, as shown for standard vinyl and wood windows.

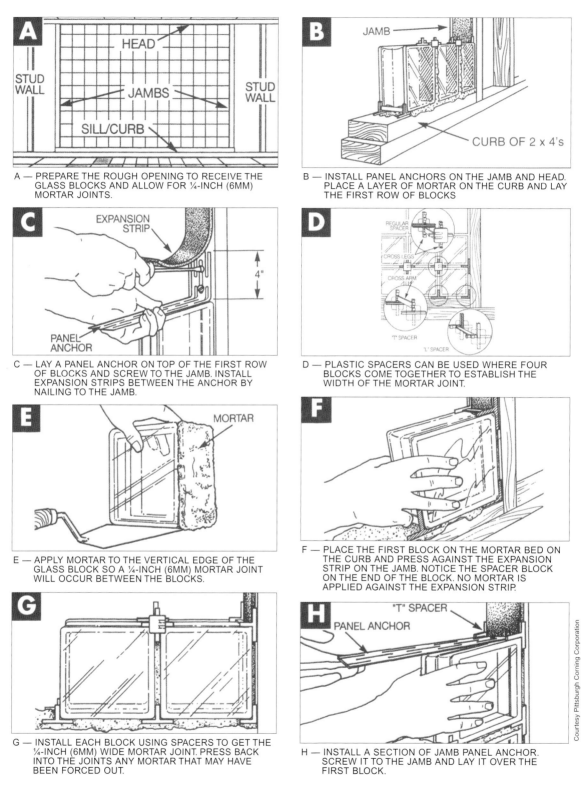

A — PREPARE THE ROUGH OPENING TO RECEIVE THE GLASS BLOCKS AND ALLOW FOR ¼-INCH (6MM) MORTAR JOINTS.

B — INSTALL PANEL ANCHORS ON THE JAMB AND HEAD. PLACE A LAYER OF MORTAR ON THE CURB AND LAY THE FIRST ROW OF BLOCKS

C — LAY A PANEL ANCHOR ON TOP OF THE FIRST ROW OF BLOCKS AND SCREW TO THE JAMB. INSTALL EXPANSION STRIPS BETWEEN THE ANCHOR BY NAILING TO THE JAMB.

D — PLASTIC SPACERS CAN BE USED WHERE FOUR BLOCKS COME TOGETHER TO ESTABLISH THE WIDTH OF THE MORTAR JOINT.

E — APPLY MORTAR TO THE VERTICAL EDGE OF THE GLASS BLOCK SO A ¼-INCH (6MM) MORTAR JOINT WILL OCCUR BETWEEN THE BLOCKS.

F — PLACE THE FIRST BLOCK ON THE MORTAR BED ON THE CURB AND PRESS AGAINST THE EXPANSION STRIP ON THE JAMB. NOTICE THE SPACER BLOCK ON THE END OF THE BLOCK. NO MORTAR IS APPLIED AGAINST THE EXPANSION STRIP.

G — INSTALL EACH BLOCK USING SPACERS TO GET THE ¼-INCH (6MM) WIDE MORTAR JOINT. PRESS BACK INTO THE JOINTS ANY MORTAR THAT MAY HAVE BEEN FORCED OUT.

H — INSTALL A SECTION OF JAMB PANEL ANCHOR. SCREW IT TO THE JAMB AND LAY IT OVER THE FIRST BLOCK.

Courtesy Pittsburgh Corning Corporation

6-50 (Above and opposite page) These steps are typical for installing glass blocks with the use of panel anchors and expansion strips on each row.

As with any window installation, you must establish the size of the rough opening. The manufacturer has tables to help with this decision. A brief summary of how to install glass blocks using white portland-cement mortar and accessories provided by one manufacturer is shown in **6-50**. Additional details are available from the manufacturer.

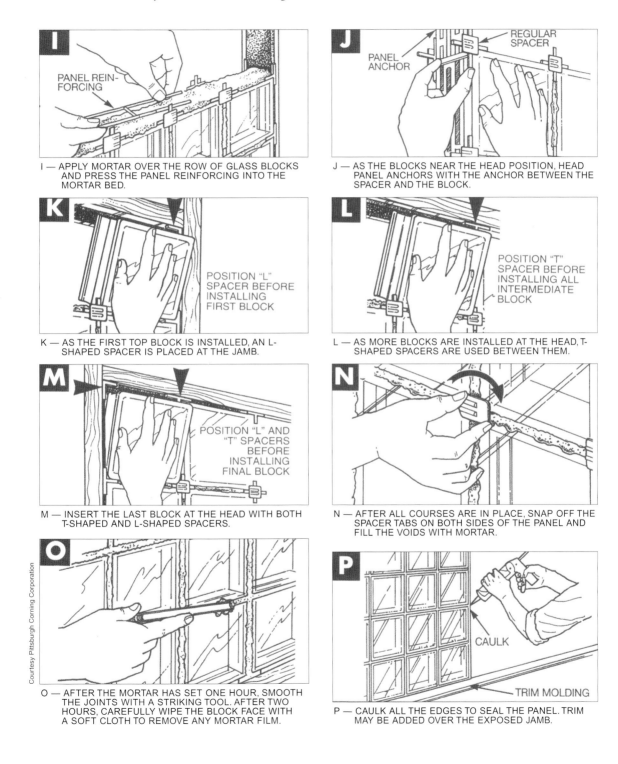

I — APPLY MORTAR OVER THE ROW OF GLASS BLOCKS AND PRESS THE PANEL REINFORCING INTO THE MORTAR BED.

J — AS THE BLOCKS NEAR THE HEAD POSITION, HEAD PANEL ANCHORS WITH THE ANCHOR BETWEEN THE SPACER AND THE BLOCK.

K — AS THE FIRST TOP BLOCK IS INSTALLED, AN L-SHAPED SPACER IS PLACED AT THE JAMB.

L — AS MORE BLOCKS ARE INSTALLED AT THE HEAD, T-SHAPED SPACERS ARE USED BETWEEN THEM.

M — INSERT THE LAST BLOCK AT THE HEAD WITH BOTH T-SHAPED AND L-SHAPED SPACERS.

N — AFTER ALL COURSES ARE IN PLACE, SNAP OFF THE SPACER TABS ON BOTH SIDES OF THE PANEL AND FILL THE VOIDS WITH MORTAR.

O — AFTER THE MORTAR HAS SET ONE HOUR, SMOOTH THE JOINTS WITH A STRIKING TOOL. AFTER TWO HOURS, CAREFULLY WIPE THE BLOCK FACE WITH A SOFT CLOTH TO REMOVE ANY MORTAR FILM.

P — CAULK ALL THE EDGES TO SEAL THE PANEL. TRIM MAY BE ADDED OVER THE EXPOSED JAMB.

Courtesy Pittsburgh Corning Corporation

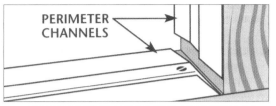

PERIMETER CHANNELS

1 — CUT THE CHANNELS TO LENGTH, AND INSTALL ON THE BOTTOM AND SIDES OF THE ROUGH OPENING WITH FLAT-HEAD GALLVANIZED SCREWS.

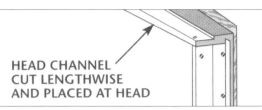

HEAD CHANNEL CUT LENGTHWISE AND PLACED AT HEAD

2 — AT THE HEAD, CUT A CHANNEL IN HALF SO THE TOP ROW CAN BE EASILY INSTALLED.

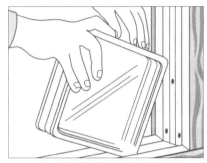

3 — PLACE GLASS BLOCKS ON THE SILL CHANNEL. PUT ONE AGAINST THE TIGHT JAMB AND OTHER AGAINST THE LEFT JAMB.

4 — INSERT THE GLASS BLOCKS BETWEEN THESE AND TAP VERTICAL SPACERS BETWEEN EACH.

5 — PLACE A HORIZONTAL SPACER ON TOP OF THE ROW. CONTINUE LAYING EACH ROW IN THIS MANNER.

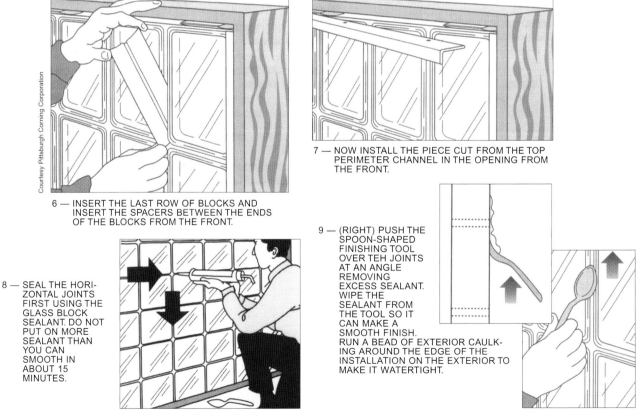

Courtesy Pittsburgh Corning Corporation

6 — INSERT THE LAST ROW OF BLOCKS AND INSERT THE SPACERS BETWEEN THE ENDS OF THE BLOCKS FROM THE FRONT.

7 — NOW INSTALL THE PIECE CUT FROM THE TOP PERIMETER CHANNEL IN THE OPENING FROM THE FRONT.

8 — SEAL THE HORIZONTAL JOINTS FIRST USING THE GLASS BLOCK SEALANT. DO NOT PUT ON MORE SEALANT THAN YOU CAN SMOOTH IN ABOUT 15 MINUTES.

9 — (RIGHT) PUSH THE SPOON-SHAPED FINISHING TOOL OVER TEH JOINTS AT AN ANGLE REMOVING EXCESS SEALANT. WIPE THE SEALANT FROM THE TOOL SO IT CAN MAKE A SMOOTH FINISH. RUN A BEAD OF EXTERIOR CAULKING AROUND THE EDGE OF THE INSTALLATION ON THE EXTERIOR TO MAKE IT WATERTIGHT.

6-51 These steps show how to install glass blocks using plastic rigid track, perimeter channels, and sealant. This is easy to do and does not require a lot of cleanup as is necessary when cement mortar is used.

INSTALLING GLASS BLOCK USING A PLASTIC TRACK SYSTEM

The **Kwikn EZ®** rigid track silicone system offered by Pittsburgh Corning Corporation makes it easier to install glass blocks than using portland-cement mortar. This system is designed for use with 3-inch (76mm) glass blocks available from the manufacturer. The manufacturer also provides the rigid track, perimeter channels, and sealant.

Begin by preparing the opening plumb and square and the size specified by the manufacturer. The installation process is detailed in the steps shown in **6-51**.

INSTALLING GLASS-BLOCK WINDOWS IN PREASSEMBLED UNITS

Frame the rough opening as described for vinyl windows. Flash the edge as shown in **6-52**. These windows consist of 8 x 8 x 3-inch (203 x 203 x 76mm) glass blocks. They are set in a vinyl frame that has welded corners. A double bead of pressure-applied silicone sealant is installed between the blocks and at the frame. The manufacturer has a wide range of sizes available.

They have a nailing fin and are installed as described for vinyl windows (**6-53**). After installation, interior trim can be applied, finishing off the window in the same manner as the other windows in the room (**6-54**).

Courtesy Pittsburgh Corning Corporation

6-52 This preassembled glass-block window is installed using nailing fins as described for standard windows. Notice the rough opening is also flashed in the same manner.

Courtesy Pittsburgh Corning Corporation

6-53 The preassembled glass-block window is placed in the rough opening, leveled, plumbed, and secured by nailing through a fin.

Courtesy Pittsburgh Corning Corporation

6-54 This finished glass-block window is cased on the inside of the house in the same manner as standard windows.

6-55 This glass-block window uses blocks 2 inches thick. This makes the assembly lighter than standard block windows. It has a vinyl frame with a nailing fin and uses a metal grid system and a silicone sealant between the rows of blocks.

Another preassembled glass-block system, mortarless **Blokup®**, is shown in **6-55**. It uses a 2-inch- (51mm) thick glass block mounted in an aluminum or vinyl frame with a nailing fin and uses metal spacers between the rows of glass blocks. They are sealed with a special sealer. It is considerably lighter than windows made with standard 3-inch (76mm) glass blocks.

These 2-inch (51mm) glass blocks can also be installed in rough openings on the site using a system of metal channels and spacers. Recommended installation procedures for the mortarless Blokup® system are shown in the steps in **6-56**.

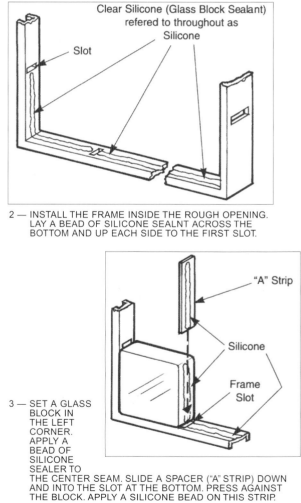

2 — INSTALL THE FRAME INSIDE THE ROUGH OPENING. LAY A BEAD OF SILICONE SEALNT ACROSS THE BOTTOM AND UP EACH SIDE TO THE FIRST SLOT.

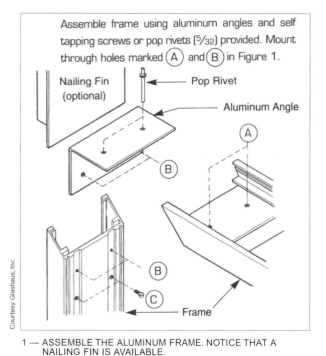

1 — ASSEMBLE THE ALUMINUM FRAME. NOTICE THAT A NAILING FIN IS AVAILABLE.

3 — SET A GLASS BLOCK IN THE LEFT CORNER. APPLY A BEAD OF SILICONE SEALER TO THE CENTER SEAM. SLIDE A SPACER ("A" STRIP) DOWN AND INTO THE SLOT AT THE BOTTOM. PRESS AGAINST THE BLOCK. APPLY A SILICONE BEAD ON THIS STRIP.

6-56 (Above and opposite page) Installation of 2-inch-thick glass blocks using the Blokup® system.

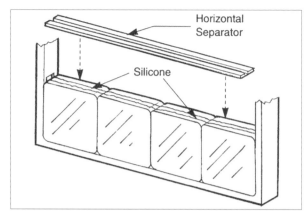

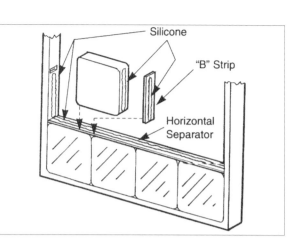

4 — REPEAT THESE STEPS AS YOU PLACE ADDITIONAL BLOCKS FORMING THE FIRST ROW. APPLY A BEAD OF SILICONE ON TOP OF THE BLOCKS AND PLACE A HORIZONTAL SEPARATOR INTO ONE END SLOT ON THE JAMB, SET ON TOP OF THE BLOCK AND SLIP IT INTO THE SLOT ON THE OTHER JAMB.

5 — APPLY A BEAD ON THE SEPARATOR STRIP AND THE JAMBS TO THE NEXT SLOT. INSTALL A BLOCK ON THE LEFT SIDE AND COMPLETE LAYING THE NEXT ROW. REPEAT UNTIL ONLY THE TOP ROW IS OPEN.

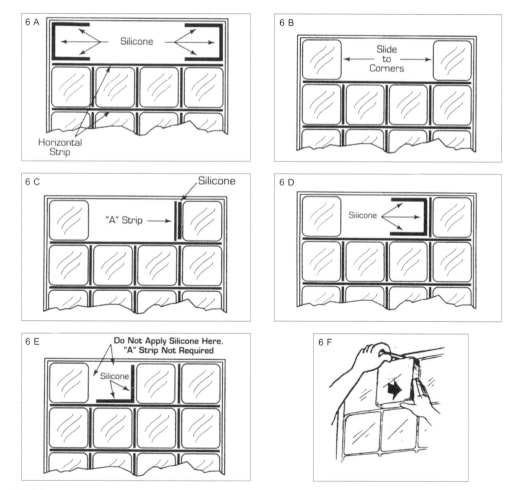

6 — APPLY SILICONE TO THE ENDS OF THE TOP OPENING AND INSTALL A BLOCK ON EACH END. INSTALL A VERTICAL SEPARATOR STRIP AND INSERT ANOTHER BLOCK. TO INSTALL THE LIST BLOCK APPLY SILICONE TO TWO SIDES AND SLIDE THE BLOCK IN THE OPENING. A SEPARATOR STRIP IS NOT NEEDED ON THE TOP OR LEFT SIDE. THIS IS FILLED WITH SILICONE SEALANT AFTER THE LAST BLOCK IS IN PLACE. CLEAN EXCESS SILICONE FROM THE GLASS FACES WITH A CLOTH MOISTENED WITH THE SOLVENT RECOMMENDED BY THE MANUFACTURER.

INSTALLING WINDOWS IN NEW CONSTRUCTION

INSTALLING BAY & BOW WINDOWS

The procedure for installing bay and bow windows is essentially the same. The manufacturers provide drawings and suggestions for installing their products, which are available in a range of heights and widths. **Bay windows** have three sash (**6-57**). The end sash are typically casement units, so they can be opened. The end sash are on an angle of 30 degrees or 45 degrees. **Bow windows** contain three to seven sash and are placed on an arc of a curve (**6-58**). See Chapter 3 for additional information.

The window must have support below it. This is typically a **wood frame** or a **cable support system**. It is also possible to construct a masonry foundation wall below it. The wall should be on the same angle or curvature as the window.

Begin by making the rough opening the size specified by the manufacturer. Check to be certain it is level and plumb. It must be solidly built to carry the weight and receive the screws and fasteners. After flashing the opening, raise the window into it and temporarily secure in place. It is heavy and will require several people to lift and hold in place. Position it so the inner edge of the frame is flush with the finish on the inside wall.

Use shims to center and square the unit. Check it for squareness before installing the permanent fasteners. Install wood screws through the headboard and seatboard into the rough-opening framing. Countersink the screw heads so they can be covered during the finishing operation. Keep the unit supported as it is installed, until the cable or other supports are in place.

Bow and bay windows receive some support from a wood frame built out below them. In **6-59** the window has a wood frame below it that provides a space for insulation. The main weight of the overhanging unit is supported by a cable that has a threaded bolt on the end. The cable is mounted to the wall above the window. The threaded rod is placed at the farthest corners of the window unit. The cable should leave the house on an angle of at least 30 degrees and 45 degrees (**6-59**).

Another method of support is to place brackets below the window. They are secured to the bottom window panel and the wall (**6-60**). The supports can be wood or metal.

Bow and bay windows can also be supported by extending the floor joists out and building a frame wall from the window to the floor (**6-61**). This also provides additional floor area.

Once the unit is in place, fill any cracks on the inside wall with loose fill insulation. Seal all external cracks with exterior caulking.

Fill the space below the seatboard with insulation and seal over the bottom with ⅜-inch (9mm) exterior plywood or some other exterior panel material.

6-57 Bay windows have three sash. Generally the side sash meet the wall on a 30-degree or 45-degree angle.

6-58 A bow window will have three to seven sash that are laid on the curve of an arc.

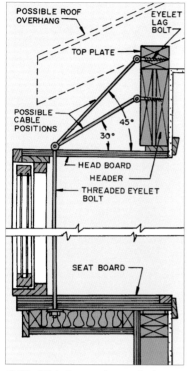

6-59 This bay or bow window is supported by the exterior wall framing. The part overhanging the wall is supported by cables.

6-60 The overhanging weight of this bow or bay window is supported by several brackets. They can be wood or metal.

6-61 Bay and bow windows can be supported by cantilevering the floor and framing below the window to the floor. Another possibility is to build a foundation below the window structure.

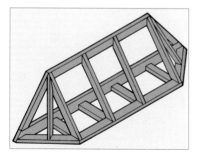

6-62 A typical way to frame a roof over a bay or bow window.

6-63 The roof can be finished with shingles to match those on the house, or some form of metal roofing can be used.

Courtesy Andersen Windows, Inc.

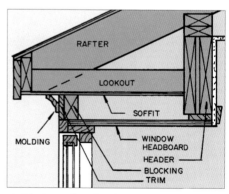

6-64 A roof with a long overhang can often be used to cover a bow or bay window.

Usually the roof overhang is not in a position to form a roof over the window.

Frame the roof structure as shown in **6-62**. The finish roofing material can be shingles to match those on the house, copper, or some type of metal roofing (**6-63**).

Should the roof have a wide overhang, the bow or bay window can be covered with it and finished something like that shown in **6-64**.

Replacement Windows & Storm Windows

O lder homes will often have inefficient, single-glazed windows with unclad wood frames and sash. They may be in a state of deterioration including rot, many layers of peeling paint, and loose putty around the glass, and may not even have weather stripping. Old metal windows do not have a thermal break and are especially big heat losers. Typically they do not close tightly, allowing considerable air infiltration and possible water leakage into the house and inside the wall. Exterior caulking may be dry and cracking, also allowing air and water penetration. The flashing may be rusted and leaking.

Some older windows may still be good enough to renovate. However, while restored to sound condition they will most likely be energy inefficient. Storm windows can be added over these old sound, inefficient windows. They protect them from the weather, increase the energy efficiency, and reduce air infiltration. However, new double-glazed windows with energy-efficient frames and sash will produce greater savings and increased comfort. If the old windows have deteriorated, it is best to replace them with energy-efficient windows. There is more information on storm windows later in this chapter.

SAVINGS

Your window dealer can possibly give you information on how much you will save each year by replacing inefficient windows. The exact amount will vary depending upon the circum-

7-1 These beautiful replacement windows renovate an old, deteriorating bow window and increase the comfort of the occupants in the dining room. They also add to the value of the house.

Courtesy Chelsea Building Products, Inc.

stances. The type and quality of the old windows and the extent of deterioration are major factors If they are single-glazed, new double-glazed energy-efficient windows can cut the heat loss almost 50 percent. This is because they not only reduce heat loss through the glazing but are tightly sealed and flashed to reduce air infiltration. This saves on both the heating and air-conditioning costs.

Savings of 15 to 20 percent are possible in many cases. Once the possible savings are determined you can figure the dollar amount per year saved and quickly see how long it will take to pay for the windows. In addition, the savings continue after you have recovered the installation costs. The replacement widows will also add some value to the house and can be considered an investment that will pay off when you sell the house (7-1).

Finally all the years that you have been more comfortable since the replacement windows were installed are difficult to give a dollar value to. Nevertheless, this is definitely a factor to be considered.

Replacement windows have low maintenance costs if they are vinyl or aluminum or wood with a vinyl covering. They are easily washed clean of mold or mildew and will last for many years.

Replacement windows are easy to open and close and have better locks than old windows. Older windows have often been painted many times and tend to stick. Some run on wood side-jamb channels that can swell and bind. Replacement windows have vinyl or aluminum channels, so will always move easily.

All of these factors have value that is real but difficult to state in terms of dollars. Generally replacement windows are a wise investment.

Courtesy Chelsea Building Products, Inc.

7-2 These replacement windows duplicate the original windows in the kitchen. They improve the overall appearance and reduce heating and cooling costs.

With careful selection of the right style replacement window, the exterior and interior appearance of the house can be enhanced. This increases the value of the house and is especially a major factor if the real estate is for sale.

SELECTING WINDOW REPLACEMENTS

The actual selection of a replacement window involves more than just getting the most energy-efficient unit. If the house has **historical significance**, the windows chosen need to replicate the original windows as closely as possible. Frequently the replacement windows will be the same type as the old windows (7-2). The original windows were not energy efficient, and one reason to replace them is to improve this condition. However, replacement windows will have double-glazing, low-E glass, and other features requiring a heavier frame and muntins to support the weight. This means they will not exactly match the sash profile of the original windows.

The U.S. Department of the Interior and many local jurisdictions have preservation standards to be met so that the architectural integrity of a historic building is maintained. This requires study of existing replacement windows available and consideration of using custom-built windows.

If historical significance is not a factor, take time to consider how various styles will influence the exterior styling. The replacement windows need not replicate the original windows. This is a time to rethink the appearance and how a change could improve interior conditions. Examine Chapter 3 for information on the types of window available.

Consider the size of the replacement window. The original appearance can be maintained if the same size windows are used. It is easier to install same-size windows because the rough opening will not have to be changed. However, do not miss a chance to put in something that will enhance the interior, such as larger windows letting in more light or opening up a room to an attractive view. Natural ventilation can also be improved by window selection. Examine Chapter 2 for information on locating windows. Information on installing replacement windows is found later in this chapter.

After the type of window to be used has been decided it is time to consider its energy efficiency. The window should usually be double glazed and the airspace filled with argon gas. The frame and sash should be energy efficient. The window should have sound construction and careful control over air infiltration, solar-heat gain, and ultraviolet transmission, yet transmit adequate natural light. Study Chapter 4 to become familiar with energy efficiency factors and Chapter 5 to get information on glazing. Look for energy-efficiency rating labels on the windows to see whether they are suitable for your climate. Review the information in Chapter 4 related to the Energy Star Climate Region Map label, the American Architectural Manufacturers Association certification label, and the National Fenestration Rating Council label. These specify the energy-related factors for the window on which the label has been placed. Not all windows are suitable for all climates.

Finally consider the cost. If you are going to do the installation yourself, visit several window dealers and get firm bids and full information on how easy or difficult it will be to install each of the window systems available. If a contractor is to be employed, first select the window you want and then get several bids that include the window and installation costs. Have on record what is included. Does the bid include screens, repairs to inside and exterior walls, painting, installing window casing, and other factors that may be involved with the situation? Is the contractor insured? Can you obtain several references? Proper installation is critical to getting the energy efficiency available from the new window.

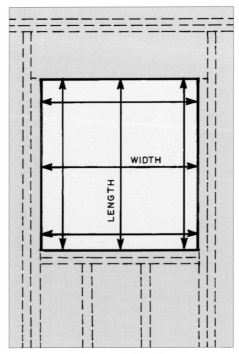

7-3 When ordering full replacement windows, measure the length and width of the rough opening in three places and order using the smallest dimension.

PREPARING TO ORDER REPLACEMENT WINDOWS

Window manufacturers have available a wide choice of replacement window systems. It is recommended that you examine the types available locally and become familiar with the installation procedures. Most replacement windows are installed by contractors who specialize in this work. The method of installation on some of the very energy-efficient units can be somewhat complex. Other units have simpler procedures and can be installed by a home owner who is skilled in the use of tools.

Replacement windows are available in **replacement sash kits** and **full window-replacement units**. A replacement sash kit is less expensive and uses the existing window frame and puts new sash on it. The full window is an assembled unit with the frame and sash ready to be installed. It generally requires that the entire old window be removed, exposing the framing of the rough opening. Some manufacturers will custom-make the windows to fit the existing opening. It is important to measure carefully when ordering all types of window.

If a full replacement window is to be used, measure the size of the rough opening as shown in 7-3. Measure as shown and use the smallest dimensions to order the window. If a sash replacement kit is to be used, measure as shown in 7-4. Here the measurements are taken from the inside of the old frame. Notice that the vertical measurements are taken to the top of the sill. The standard sill angle is 14 degrees.

If the replacement window is to be larger or smaller than the window to be replaced, the framing for the rough opening must be changed. This is discussed later in this chapter.

Replacement windows are available in a large range of standard sizes. The standardization of the window sizes usually means that only minor adjustments in the opening are needed.

Windows are available in wood, wood clad in vinyl or aluminum, solid vinyl, and composite. Be certain to check on the manufacturer's warranty. If a contractor is installing them, see what type of warranty is offered for the installation labor costs.

INSTALLING REPLACEMENT WINDOWS

There are many types of replacement window on the market. Manufacturers have instruction manuals and videotapes to help assure they are installed correctly. Be certain to study these materials because there are major differences in how various windows and brands are installed. Correct installation is critical to the ultimate operation of and satisfaction with the new window. In this chapter several systems will be presented.

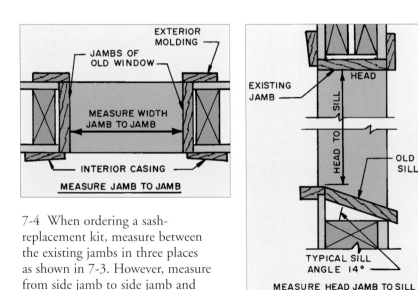

7-4 When ordering a sash-replacement kit, measure between the existing jambs in three places as shown in 7-3. However, measure from side jamb to side jamb and head jamb to sill.

PREPARING THE ROUGH OPENING

As you plan to install a full replacement window, be aware that it fits into an opening in the wall framed with structural members. This opening is called the **rough opening**. The rough opening is typically ½ inch (13mm) larger than the overall unit size. Typical framing for a rough opening is seen in 7-5. The header is a structural member that spans the rough opening and carries any load above the window such as ceiling joists or second floor joists. A second wall stud, called a trimmer stud, is on each side. A double sill forms the bottom of the rough opening.

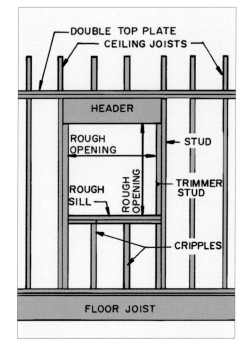

7-5 A typical rough opening for a window has a header across the top to carry the overhead load. Trimmer studs support it. The bottom of the rough opening is framed with a sill.

CHANGING THE SIZE

If the replacement window is to be smaller or larger than the window it is to replace, the framing for the rough opening will have to be altered.

The size of the rough opening depends upon the replacement window. Manufacturers specify the rough-opening size for each window.

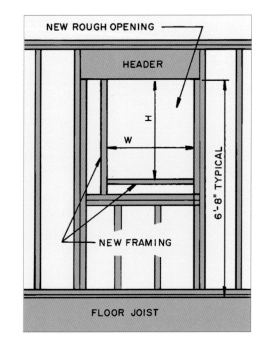

7-6 Typical framing for making the rough opening smaller.

ADJUSTING FOR A SMALLER WINDOW

Begin by removing the old window and frame, exposing the framing of the rough opening. This will include removing the interior window casing and possibly exterior molding around the window or sometimes some of the siding. Then install studs and a sill in the rough opening as shown in 7-6. The window can be lowered in the wall by framing a member below the header. However, the tops of windows are typically 6 feet 8 inches above the floor so that they align with the tops of the doors.

ADJUSTING FOR A LARGER WINDOW

The framing for a larger window is more difficult. Since the width of the rough opening is larger than the existing header, a new, longer header is required. Since the old header is supporting an overhead ceiling or floor, this weight must be supported before the old header is removed. This can be done by installing a temporary partition below the ceiling joists as shown in 7-7. Be certain the floor is strong enough to carry the load.

Under normal conditions the bottom plate on the temporary partition will spread the load over several floor joists. If there is any doubt about the strength of the floor joists, install a temporary beam below the floor. It can be supported on concrete blocks laid without mortar (7-8).

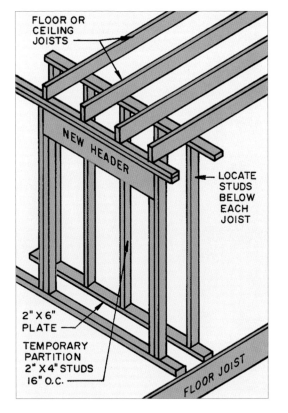

7-7 A temporary partition can be built to support the overhead joists as the old header is removed and the new, longer one is installed.

It is also possible that the temporary partition may cause minor damage to the ceiling material, so repairs may be necessary. You might pad the top plate with a piece of carpet.

After a temporary beam has been postioned on concrete blocks and any necessary shimming for support below the floor and the temporary partition, as needed, has been put in place, you are ready to remove the old header as well as any unneeded studs, sill, and cripples. This will involve cutting away drywall on the interior wall and cutting back the exterior siding. Careful measuring is important so that too much material is not cut away. If this happens, it will require some extra patching after the window is in place.

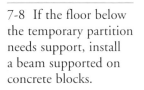

7-8 If the floor below the temporary partition needs support, install a beam supported on concrete blocks.

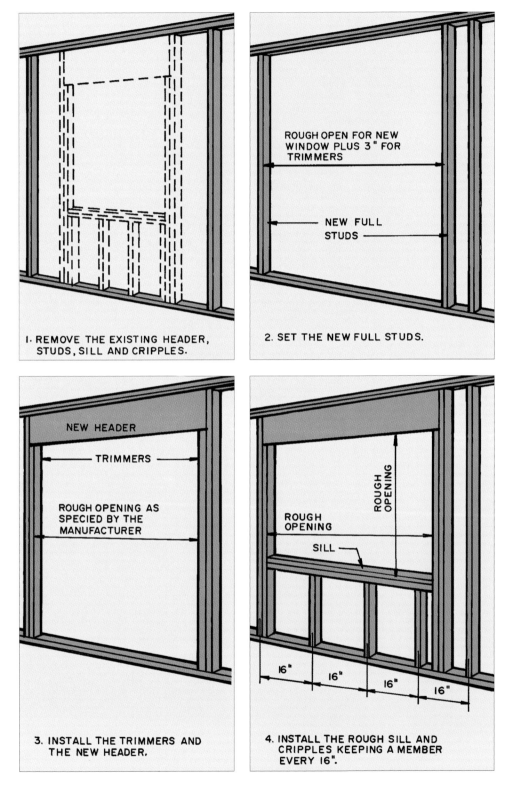

1. REMOVE THE EXISTING HEADER, STUDS, SILL AND CRIPPLES.

ROUGH OPEN FOR NEW WINDOW PLUS 3" FOR TRIMMERS

NEW FULL STUDS

2. SET THE NEW FULL STUDS.

NEW HEADER

TRIMMERS

ROUGH OPENING AS SPECIED BY THE MANUFACTURER

3. INSTALL THE TRIMMERS AND THE NEW HEADER.

ROUGH OPENING

ROUGH OPENING

SILL

16" 16" 16" 16"

4. INSTALL THE ROUGH SILL AND CRIPPLES KEEPING A MEMBER EVERY 16".

7-9 Typical framing for a larger rough opening.

Now frame the new rough opening as shown in 7-9. Always have a stud or cripple every 16 inches on center. This is necessary so that a nailer for the drywall is available every 16 inches.

Since the opening to be spanned is larger than the original, consider the size of the new header. In 7-10 are two designs widely used.

To install the replacement window, make sure that you follow the manufacturer's directions. Procedures vary depending upon the type of window to be installed as well as upon the brand of window to be used. Most replacement windows are designed so that they can be installed from the inside of the wall.

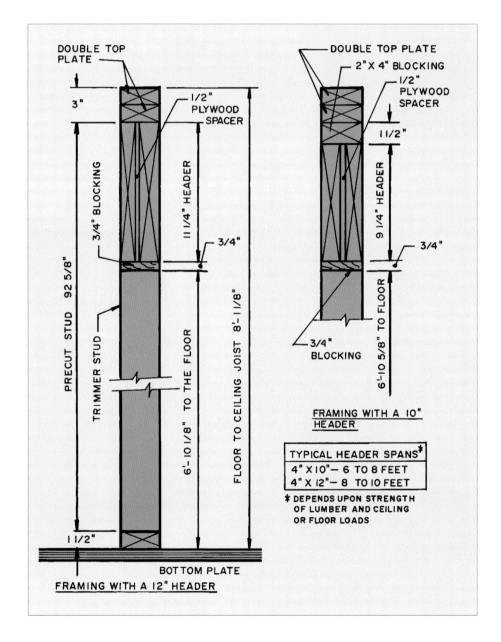

7-10 Two header designs frequently used to span wide window openings.

KITS TO REPLACE THE SASH

Old houses have double-hung windows that are balanced by weights hanging on a cord that runs over pulleys set in the window frame. A good window system that replaces the cord and weights with vinyl jamb liners and new sash is shown in **7-11**. This replacement window has vinyl jamb liners with weather stripping. The upper and lower sash slide in the jamb liners. This replacement window is available in a wide range of sizes, making it easy to fit most rough openings with no or very little change.

To order the replacement window, carefully measure the width and height (**7-12** and **7-3**). Then from the sizes available select

7-11 This is a sash replacement kit. The jamb liners are installed on the inside of the old window frame and the new sash are inserted into the jamb liners.

7-12 Measure the width between the faces of the side jambs and from the head jamb to the sill at a point where the outside face of the bottom sash touches the sill when it is closed.

Courtesy Kolbe and Kolbe Millwork Co., Inc.

the one that fits the opening. If necessary, install a thin wood piece on the jamb to adjust the width of the opening.

Installation procedures for the replacement window in **7-11** begin by removing the old window as shown in **7–13** through **7-16**. Once the old window sash, stops, cord, weights, and pulleys are removed and only the frame and the clear opening are left, you are ready to begin installing the replacement window.

7-13 Carefully remove the sash stops with a putty knife or pry bar. Save them because they will be reapplied after installation of the replacement sash.

7-14 Lift out the bottom sash. If it has the rope-and-pulley operation, cut the rope and remove the pulleys and counterweights.

7-15 Remove the side parting stops and discard them. Now remove the upper sash, cut the rope, and remove the pulleys and counterweights.

7-16 Remove the head parting strip and discard it.

7-18 Slide the vinyl sash stops into the top inside track of each jamb liner.

7-17 Nail the jamb-liner clips to the frame. Space as specified in the directions by the manufacturer.

7-19 Apply the self-sticking foam pads to each jamb-liner head.

7-20 Snap the jamb liner over the clips in the old window frame.

7-21 Reinstall the wood parting strip at the head and cover it with a vinyl parting strip.

7-22 Insert the upper sash in the jamb liner as per instructions and raise it to the top of the frame.

Begin by installing the clips holding the jamb-liner in place (7-17). Install the sash stops and end pad as shown in 7-18 and 7-19. Now snap the jamb liner in place over the jamb liner clips (7-20) and install the head parting strip (7-21). Insert the top sash into the jamb liner and insert a clutch pivot above the clutch in the track. Lay it flat and press the jamb liner while pushing the sash into the track. Raise the sash to the top position (7-22). Repeat the steps to install the lower sash (7-23). Finally, replace the original sash stops (7-24).

7-23 (Above and above right) Repeat the installation steps for the lower sash.

7-24 Reinstall the original sash stops. If they were damaged, replace them with new stops.

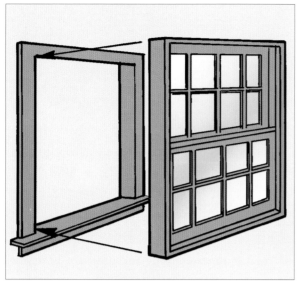

7-25 This pocket window is a completely assembled unit ready to install inside the jambs of the old window.

INSTALLING A POCKET WINDOW

A pocket window is a completely assembled window with a frame and sash ready to install in a window opening after the old window has been removed. If the old window is a wood unit, it is removed as shown earlier in **7-13** through **7-15**. Remove the old stops and sash, and cut the sash cord or chain. If the frame is in good condition, the pocket window is slid into the opening and secured as directed by the manufacturer (**7-25**). The installation is made from the inside of the room and the existing window casing is not disturbed (**7-26**).

7-26 The pocket window is installed from the inside of the room.

7-27 This pocket window is easily installed from inside the house and is available in many sizes.

7-28 After caulking as directed by the manufacturer, install one screw in an upper corner.

7-29 After installing a screw in one corner, check the unit for level and plumb.

This discussion presents general techniques and does not cover all instructions possible for a pocket window installation. The window manufacturer will provide instructions needed to install its window. The procedures and fastening recommendations will have numerous differences.

A pocket replacement window that is fully assembled is shown in **7-27**. It is of all-vinyl construction, therefore requiring no maintenance. These are custom-made to fit the exact window opening.

After the old window sash has been removed and the old frame found to be sound or been repaired, the new window can be slid into the opening for a trial fit. If it fits properly, remove the window and caulk the opening as directed by the instructions.

Reinsert the window and install one screw in the upper end of one jamb (**7-28**). Check for level and plumb (**7-29**). Use wedges to adjust as necessary but do not drive them too tight or the frame may be bowed, causing the sliding sash to stick. Place a wedge at the location for each screw to be installed through the frame (**7-30**).

Courtesy Weather Shield Windows & Doors

7-30 Use shims where necessary to hold the unit level and plumb.

REPLACEMENT WINDOWS & STORM WINDOWS

7-31 After installing shims and a screw in the other upper corner, check the diagonals to be certain the unit is square.

7-33 Acrylic-block replacement windows are assembled in a vinyl frame.

7-32 Lower the inside sash near the sill and measure the distance between them in several places. This measurement should be the same distance across the sill.

7-34 This retrofit acrylic-block window installation uses casement windows.

When it is level and plumb, install the top screw on the other jamb. Now measure across the diagonals as shown in **7-31**. If these distances are equal, the frame is square. If not, adjust with the wedges until it is square.

Now lower the sash until it is just above the sill. Measure the distance between the sash and sill as shown in **7-32**. These distances should be the same. If all is level and plumb, install the remaining screws as directed by the manufacturer. Raise and lower the sash to make certain they are moving smoothly.

The manufacturer will often provide a frame extender that is used to cover any crack between the frame of the new window and the frame or sill of the old window.

In all cases be certain to caulk all seams. If the old window had the weights and pully system, remove the interior window casing and fill the weight cavity with insulation.

Remember, installation procedures will vary depending upon the design of the replacement window. These procedures are typical of those recommended.

Another type of replacement window consists of acrylic blocks mounted in a vinyl frame (**7-33**). They are manufactured in ¼-inch increments, so they can be ordered to fit almost any opening. They can also be made to fit the dimensions of any special openings. They are available in fixed, casement, awning, and hopper styles (**7-34**).

STORM WINDOWS

A storm window is a glazed unit installed on the exterior over an existing standard window or on the inside of the window. It is not really made for storms, but is used to provide increased energy efficiency and reduce air infiltration. Storm windows are useful in all climates because they reduce heat loss and gain through energy-inefficient windows. If low-E glazing is used, their efficiency is increased. A true storm window is made of impact-resistant glass and a strong aluminum frame. It is used in areas where hurricanes and other storms produce high winds and blowing debris. Information is in Chapter 5.

INTERIOR STORM WINDOWS
One way to inexpensively make **interior storm windows** is to purchase sheets of acrylic glazing and cut them to fit over the sash and screw them to the sash (**7-35**). Screw the glazing to the inside of the lower sash and to the outside of the upper sash. This allows the sash to operate, providing ventilation and emergency exit. Both sash are double glazed, reducing heat loss and gain, but air infiltration around the edges is not blocked.

PLASTIC GLAZING SECURED TO THE OUTSIDE OF THE UPPER SASH.

PLASTIC GLAZING SECURED TO THE INSIDE OF THE LOWER SASH.

7-35 One way to improve the energy efficiency of old single-glazed windows is to install sheets of plastic glazing material over the sash.

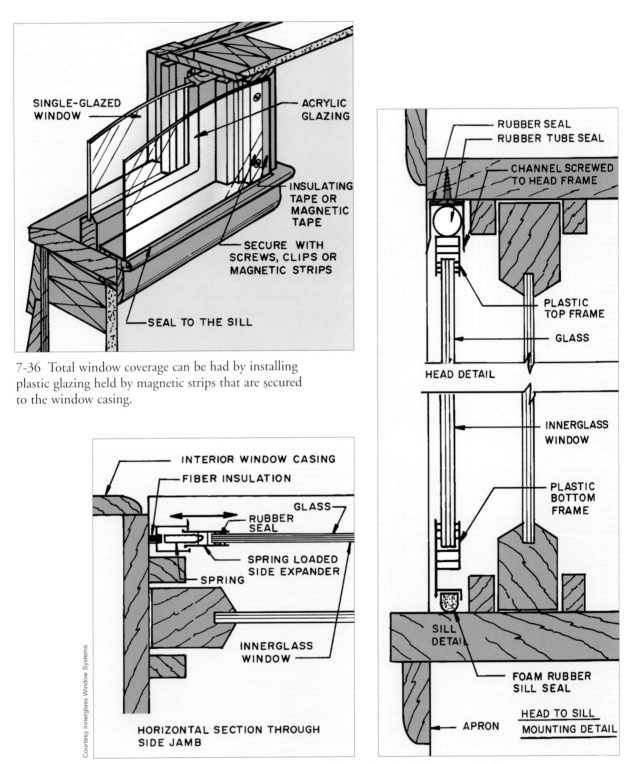

SINGLE-GLAZED WINDOW

ACRYLIC GLAZING

INSULATING TAPE OR MAGNETIC TAPE

SECURE WITH SCREWS, CLIPS OR MAGNETIC STRIPS

SEAL TO THE SILL

7-36 Total window coverage can be had by installing plastic glazing held by magnetic strips that are secured to the window casing.

RUBBER SEAL
RUBBER TUBE SEAL

CHANNEL SCREWED TO HEAD FRAME

PLASTIC TOP FRAME

GLASS

HEAD DETAIL

INNERGLASS WINDOW

PLASTIC BOTTOM FRAME

FOAM RUBBER SILL SEAL

SILL DETAIL

APRON

HEAD TO SILL MOUNTING DETAIL

INTERIOR WINDOW CASING

FIBER INSULATION

GLASS

RUBBER SEAL

SPRING LOADED SIDE EXPANDER

SPRING

INNERGLASS WINDOW

Courtesy Innerglass Window Systems

HORIZONTAL SECTION THROUGH SIDE JAMB

7-37 These details show how a vinyl-framed glass-glazed inside storm window fits against the window frame. It is easily installed and removed.

Check with the local building-supply dealer for commercially available inside storm windows. Some types have a magnetic strip around the edge of the plastic glazing and a thin metallic tape that is permanently installed to the window frame. The glazing is held to the window by the magnetic strip (7-36). Another type uses clips on the frame to hold the plastic glazing. Both of these can be easily removed when the need arises.

Another window system that increases the efficiency of older inefficient windows is a vinyl-framed, glass interior window designed to be mounted on the inside of the stops of the primary window. It seals against them, eliminating drafts and air infiltration into the airspace between it and the original window glazing. This eliminates condensation. Details showing the head and sill and side mounting are in 7-37.

The window is custom-made to fit each window. It is installed by placing the head against the frame and sliding it in place. The spring-loaded sides hold it firmly in place (7-38). The side frame is secured to the window frame with a latch on each side.

EXTERIOR STORM WINDOWS
Exterior storm windows are mounted by their flanges to the window frame (7-39). When caulked effectively, they seal the perimeter so that it is free of air leakage.

Courtesy Innerglass Window Systems

7-38 The spring-loaded frame makes installing these inside storm windows easy.

7-39 Exterior storm windows are mounted by screwing the flange to the window frame.

Exterior storm windows are usually operable having two or three tracks. **Two-track storm windows** are available for protecting vertically moving windows and horizontally sliding windows with two sash. One setup available has a screen and sash in one track and a movable sash in the other (7-40).

Triple-track storm windows have the screen and each sash in individual tracks (7-41). This allows the screen to be kept stored on the frame by sliding it up to the top of the frame and allows the top opening to be used for ventilation.

Fixed storm-window panels are available. They are usually used on large glazed areas, such as a picture window. They do not permit ventilation, and need to be removed occasionally for window maintenance.

The **frame** and **sash** are made of aluminum, which is strong and maintenance free. The **glazing** may be glass or acrylic glazing material. The **screen** may be aluminum or plastic. Aluminum screen is tough but will dent. Plastic will not dent, but will stretch and breaks more easily. Copper and stainless-steel screens are good on coastal areas because they resist corrosion better than aluminum.

When choosing a storm window for energy efficiency, note that those made by an American Architectural Manufacturers Association (AAMA) manufacturer or certified by the National Fenestration Rating Council (NFRC) will have performance ratings for each type of window. Review Chapter 4 for information on energy-efficiency ratings.

Storm windows are usually made by local manufacturers who will measure the windows and make them to fit. They provide allowances to overlap the window casing, permitting the windows to be screwed in place.

Exterior storm windows are relatively easy to install. Center the storm window over the prime window opening and install one screw in a predrilled hole at a top corner. Adjust it so it is level and install a screw in the other corner. Install screws along each side, working toward the bottom. Then lower the bottom extender piece to the sill and screw as provided. Be careful that the sides are not bowed inward, or the units will not slide. Move them as the installation proceeds to check the movement.

After the screws are in place, lay a small bead of caulking along the edge of the aluminum frame where it touches the wood window casing.

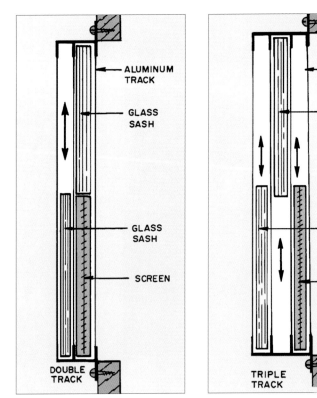

7-40 Two-track exterior storm windows have one sash that can open and a second that fits over a screen.

7-41 Triple-track storm windows allow both glazed sash to move even when the screen is installed.

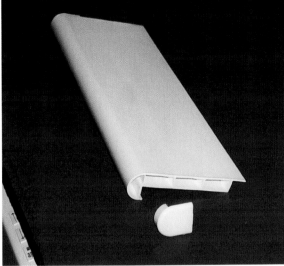

7-42 This is a sample of a vinyl replacement windowsill. It is easy to install and requires no maintenance.

A storm window will often cause an increase in the humidity and temperature between it and the prime window. This can cause damage to either wood or vinyl window frames. The higher temperatures could be especially damaging to vinyl windows and the humidity to wood windows. It is recommended that exterior storm windows have several vents to permit air exchange.

VINYL WINDOWSILLS

If the interior windowsills are old, cracked, and covered with many coats of paint, it would be wise to replace them. You can buy wood windowsills from the building supply dealer.

7-43 The installed vinyl windowsill provides a permanent, attractive replacement for deteriorated wood sills.

Another quality product is an all-vinyl windowsill (7-42). It is available in a range of widths. To install, remove the old sill and repair any damage to the rough sill below the window. Cut the vinyl sill to length with a hacksaw or fine-tooth saber saw. Smooth the cut ends with sandpaper on a flat block of wood. Then caulk the end caps and insert in each end. Now trowel a layer of solvent or latex tile mastic on the bottom of the vinyl sill and press in place. Caulk any exposed open edges. The finished installation will always be durable (7-43).

Skylights & Roof Windows

Skylights and roof windows have been used for many years to provide interior lighting in dark areas and create dramatic and pleasing interior decorative effects (**8-1**). Early units were either site-built or were rather inefficient commercially made units. With the increased emphasis on energy-efficient design, the products have been improved and have become a part of the overall energy-efficient considerations as a house is designed. Current skylights

Courtesy Andersen Windows, Inc.

8-1 Second-floor rooms in 1½-story houses can have good natural light and ventilation by using skylights and roof windows.

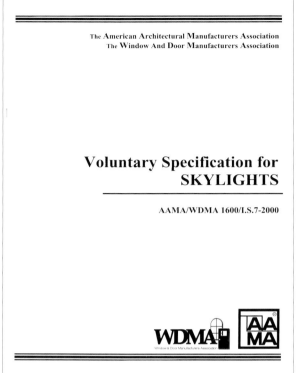

The American Architectural Manufacturers Association
The Window And Door Manufacturers Association

Voluntary Specification for SKYLIGHTS

AAMA/WDMA 1600/I.S.7-2000

WDMA
Window & Door Manufacturers Association

AAMA

8-2 This publication sets forth an extensive set of specifications for the manufacture of skylights and roof windows.

and roof windows have double glazing and energy-efficient curbs with special designed flashing. While they still provide interior illumination, they can admit solar energy in the winter to provide heat and, with energy-efficient glazing, reduce heat loss.

Cooling costs can be reduced using skylights and roof windows that open. Since heat rises, it collects along the ceiling, and by opening the unit this summer heat buildup can be vented to the outside. Therefore the role of skylights and use of roof windows in design of the house has expanded so that they have become a regular part of the overall fenestration design. The results of natural lighting, solar heat, and ventilation can serve to reduce the amount of energy required for heating and cooling.

TERMS

The terms "skylight" and "roof window" have evolved over a period of years. Often they are used interchangeably to describe a glazed opening in a roof. The actual description varies from manufacturer to manufacturer and among professional organizations. Basically both are sloped applications of a fenestration product that allows natural lighting. Some open, providing ventilation. One type pivots in the center of the sash and is used low on the roof slope where it can be opened and cleaned from within the room.

SPECIFICATIONS

The American Architectural Manufacturers Association (AAMA) and the Window and Door Manufacturers Association (WDMA) have cooperatively developed and researched specifications for the manufacture of skylights. These are published in the manual *Voluntary Specifications for Skylights, AAMA/WDMA 1600/1.S.7-2000* (8-2). It includes general requirements, performance classifications, material and component requirements, and performance requirements.

ENERGY EFFICIENCY

Some skylights have single or double layers of acrylic glazing, and roof windows have single and double layers of glass. Double-glazed units may have argon gas in the airspace and use low-E coatings. These products are the same as used in standard windows. More information on glazing is in Chapter 5.

Other factors to consider are the efficiency of the window curb and the effectiveness of the seals on operating windows to reduce air infiltration. These and other efficiency topics are discussed in Chapter 4.

CONDENSATION

Sometimes condensation will form on the interior of skylights and roof windows. This occurs when interior air has a high humidity and it strikes the glazing, which is colder than the dew point of the air. Since the air cannot hold the moisture (a vapor), it condenses into a liquid and drips off the glass or forms a frost if the glass temperature is below freezing.

Single-glazed windows are much more likely to form condensation and frost than double-glazed, energy-efficient windows because the surface temperature of the double-glazed panes tends to be warmer.

If condensation is a problem on existing windows, take action to reduce the humidity level of the interior air. Additional information on condensation is given in Chapter 1.

CLIMATE & ORIENTATION

Skylights and roof windows have the same problems and advantages as standard windows when it comes to locating them in relation to the sun and prevailing winds. In the northern hemisphere, exposure to the north provides a softer natural light; exposure to the south produces more light that is harsh, also producing more glare from the direct penetration of the suns rays. Eastern and

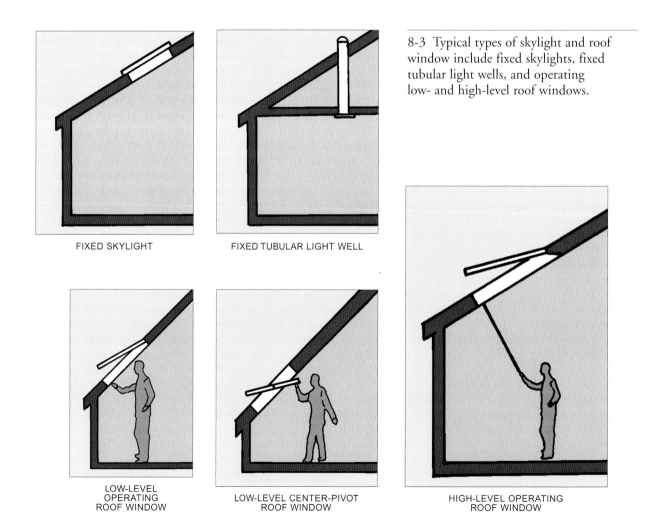

FIXED SKYLIGHT

FIXED TUBULAR LIGHT WELL

LOW-LEVEL
OPERATING
ROOF WINDOW

LOW-LEVEL CENTER-PIVOT
ROOF WINDOW

HIGH-LEVEL OPERATING
ROOF WINDOW

8-3 Typical types of skylight and roof window include fixed skylights, fixed tubular light wells, and operating low- and high-level roof windows.

western exposures provide a range of light levels as the sun appears to move across the sky as the earth rotates on its axis. The eastern exposure gives direct sunlight in the morning and the western gives direct sunlight exposure in the afternoon.

With respect to the United States, exposure also varies depending upon the region: northern, central, or southern. Additional details are in Chapter 2.

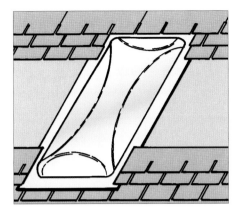

8-4 The relatively inexpensive curbless acrylic skylights are secured to the roof sheathing and are self-flashing as the roof shingling is applied directly over the edge of the skylight bubble.

lowered by activating electric controls. **Pleated shades** can provide a soft filtered light to enter the room. They have an energy-efficient coating that reflects solar heat in the summer and in the winter helps control heat loss through the window. They are available with manual and electric controls. Some electric controls are not only operated by a mounted control button but have a remote control.

SUN-SCREENING

Some skylight and roof-window manufacturers produce a number of different types of internally mounted blind and shade. **Venetian blinds** can be raised and lowered manually or with electrical controls. They help control the admission of natural light and solar energy, help with temperature control, and afford privacy. **Roller** shades control incoming natural light and reduce heat loss through the glazing. They rise and lower with a pull cord. A shade that blocks the sun can be used when complete darkness is required. This type of shade has an energy-efficient coating that reflects excessive heat from the sun. It is raised and

TYPES OF SKYLIGHT & ROOF WINDOW

Residential skylights and roof windows fall into two general types: fixed and operating. The operating roof window units may be hinged on the top or pivoted at the center of the sash (8-3).

The lowest-cost unit is a fixed **curbless acrylic bubble** (8-4). It is mounted to the sheathing and is self-flashing as shingles are applied directly over the single- or double-glazed edge of the bubble (8-5). Since the bubbles do not have a curb, they may leak during heavy rains or melting snows. The curbless skylights are more effective on steeply sloped roofs that have good drainage.

8-5 Self-flashing acrylic skylights may be single- or double-glazed.

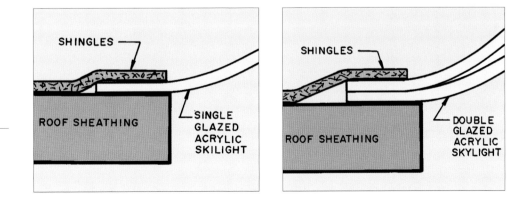

The **acrylic dome skylight mounted on a curb** (**8-6**) produces a watertight installation because the curb can be effectively sealed with metal flashing (**8-7**). It is recommended that curb-mounted bubbles have double-layer acrylic glazing, which is more energy efficient. The bubbles are available clear or with color tints. An acrylic dome curb-mounted self-flashing operating roof window is shown in **8-8**. The unit is available with either manual or electric opening controls. Typical installation details are in **8-9**.

Another unit is a curbed **mounted fixed skylight** (**8-10**). This unit has a sash similar to that used on standard windows and is glazed with one or two layers of glass. The glass is the same as used on standard windows and may be tinted, have a low-E coating, or be laminated glass to protect from storm damage. See Chapter 5 for information on glazing materials. The sash and frame are assembled into a single unit (**8-11**). The frame forms the curb. The manufacturer supplies the metal flashing. There are many variations to the actual design.

Operable roof windows have the added advantage of providing ventilation. Since hot air rises, it collects along the ceiling. The operable roof window will vent it to the outside (**8-12**).

Turning a handle at the bottom of the window (**8-13**) opens operable windows placed low on the wall or roof. The sash is moved open from the bottom by rods that pivot outward (**8-14**).

A generalized detail for an operating roof window is shown in **8-15**. The window frame forms the curb as it joins the roof. The sash is double-glazed and is wood covered with a vinyl or aluminum sheath. The frame, sash, and glazing are preassembled into a single unit.

8-6 This aluminum-framed acrylic pyramid skylight is mounted on a curb.

8-8 This is an operating curb-mounted, self-flashing acrylic roof window.

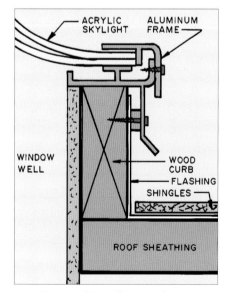

8-7 A typical installation of a curb-mounted, aluminum-framed acrylic skylight.

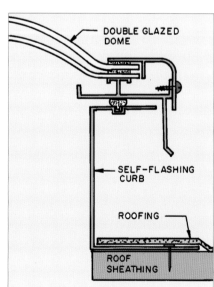

8-9 A typical installation detail for an operating self-flashing, curb-mounted acrylic roof window.

8-10 This fixed double-glazed energy-efficient skylight has a sash similar to standard windows. The sash is aluminum-clad. It is mounted on a curb as shown in 8-11.

8-12 Operable roof windows are hinged at the top. This provides a means for ventilating the room as well as admitting natural light.

8-13 A crank controls operable roof windows low on the roof.

8-14 The roof-window crank operates gears that move the sash out with control rods.

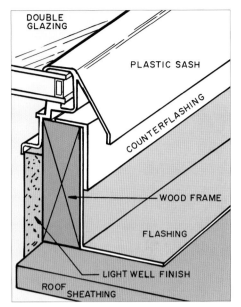

DOUBLE GLAZING
PLASTIC SASH
COUNTERFLASHING
WOOD FRAME
FLASHING
LIGHT WELL FINISH
ROOF SHEATHING

8-11 Generalized detail of a fixed skylight having a sash and frame. The frame serves as the curb and is flashed.

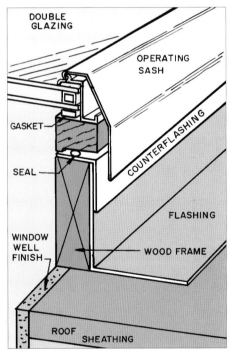

DOUBLE GLAZING
OPERATING SASH
GASKET
COUNTERFLASHING
SEAL
FLASHING
WINDOW WELL FINISH
WOOD FRAME
ROOF SHEATHING

8-15 Generalized detail of an operating roof window. The sash has a wood frame much like that on a standard window. The frame is typically vinyl- or aluminum-clad and serves as the curb.

Very high operating roof windows are opened using a long control rod to revolve the crank or have a motarized control.

Another type of operating roof window pivots in the center (**8-16**). It is located low on the roof so it can be manually operated. The sash has a lock at the top that is released and the top is pulled into the room.

Skylights and roof windows are the major source of natural light and ventilation for rooms on the second floor of one-and-a-half-story houses. The rafters form a sloped side wall and the installation of these windows is the way to provide these necessary features as seen earlier in **8-1**.

An interesting approach is to install a balcony roof window. The floor is extended to the exterior wall, widening the room. The top sash opens, providing ventilation, and pivots inward for cleaning. The bottom sash opens outward, creating a balcony and providing needed protection against falls (**8-17**).

Another way to provide considerable natural light, some extra floor space, and a view from rooms on the second floor of a one-and-a-half-story house is to install a section of a sunroom. The unit in **8-18** is installed in an opening cut in the roof and framed much like that for a large skylight.

A **tubular skylight** is a variation of skylight with a light well that is often used to admit natural light into a room (**8-19**). Basically the unit consists of a round acrylic dome mounted in a metal tube secured to flashing.

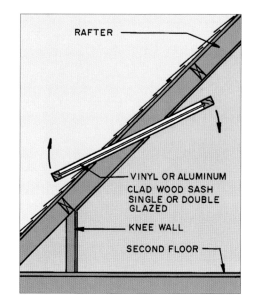

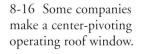

8-16 Some companies make a center-pivoting operating roof window.

The light is brought into the room through the metal tube, which can be angled as needed to go around obstacles in the attic and move the light to the location in the ceiling where it is needed (**8-20**). The tube has a reflective, mirror-like interior surface that transmits almost all of the light even when the tube is angled. The unit is easier to install than conventional skylights and roof windows.

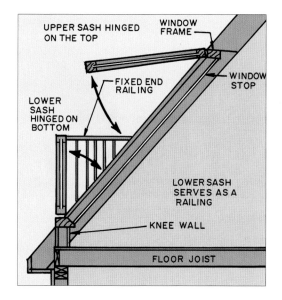

8-17 The top sash opens up, providing ventilation. The lower sash hinges out at the bottom, providing a balcony railing. The end railing is fixed.

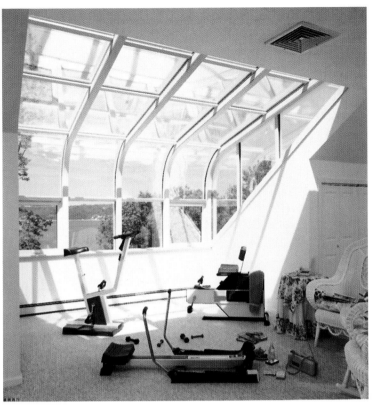

Courtesy Four Seasons Solar Products Corporation

8-18 A sunroom can be installed in the roof over rooms on the second floor of a one-and-one-half-story house. This opens up the room and makes it more enjoyable.

Courtesy Solatube International, Inc.

8-19 Tubular skylights provide considerable natural light, enhancing the lighting and providing an interesting architectural feature.

8-20 The light tube can be angled to miss obstructions in the attic or you may adjust the location of the bubble on the roof or the diffuser on the ceiling.

Courtesy Solatube International, Inc.

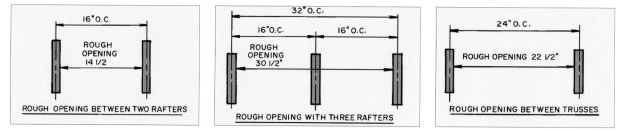

8-21 Rough openings between typical rafter and truss-framed roofs.

INSTALLING SKYLIGHTS & ROOF WINDOWS

Framing for skylight and roof window installation includes preparing the rough opening in the roof and the opening in the ceiling and building light shafts where they are required. There are two relatively straightforward procedures that are easy to do on new construction. When adding a skylight to an existing house, a great deal of measuring and planning is necessary to find the location on the roof, the postion of the light shaft, and their relation to the opening that must be cut in the existing ceiling.

The rough opening required in the roof will be specified by the window manufacturer. This varies some from one company to another. Some windows are made to fit between rafters that are

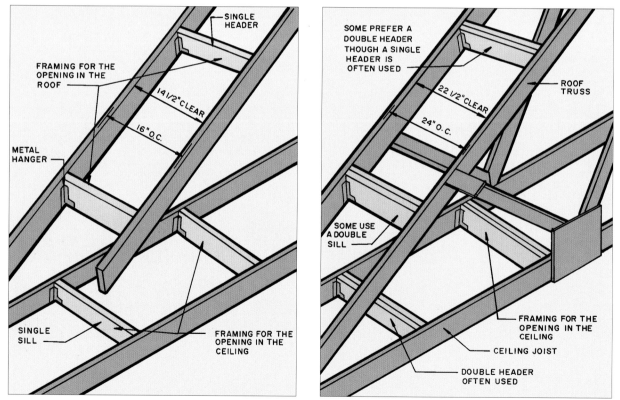

8-22 Typical roof framing for a skylight or roof window that will fit between the rafters.

8-23 Typical roof framing of a single skylight or roof window that will fit between the roof trusses.

spaced 16 inches on center and trusses spaced 24 inches on center (**8-21**). These can be installed without cutting a rafter. A window with a required rough opening of 14½ inches will slip in place if the rafters are installed at 16 inches on center. Windows for truss construction typically are made 21½ or 22 inches wide. Another frequently used size window requires a rough opening of at least 30½ inches. This will fit between rafters spaced 16 inches on center (**8-21**), but one rafter has to be cut. Never use this size with a truss-framed roof, because you must not ever cut a truss. This structurally damages the truss and, even if framed with headers, it will not carry the designed roof load.

Typical framing for installing a narrow skylight between rafters is shown in **8-22**. Since the span is small, a single header on each end establishing the length of the rough opening is generally used. Framing for a skylight between trusses is shown in **8-23**. A double header is recommended.

If you want to install a skylight that requires a rafter to be cut, double headers are used. If the opening is wider than 14½ inches but somewhat smaller than 30½ inches, frame the opening as shown in **8-24**. If a 30½-inch window is used, the framing will appear as shown in **8-25**. Notice that in both cases the rafters on each side are doubled. These are referred to as sister rafters.

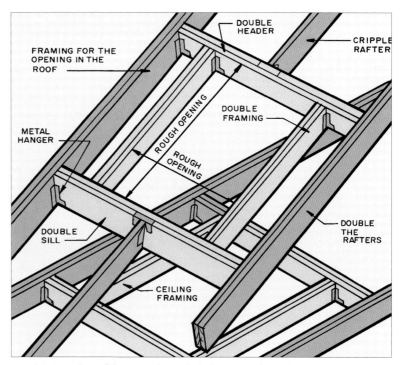

8-24 Typical roof framing for a skylight or roof window that is wider than 14½ inches but that requires less than a 30½-inch rough opening.

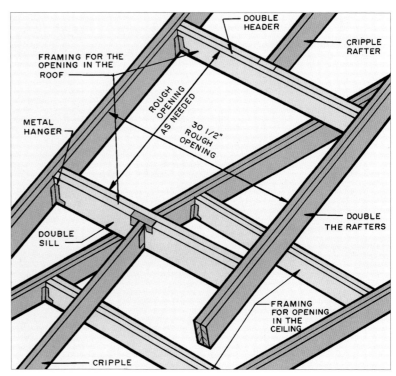

8-25 Typical roof framing for a skylight or roof window requiring the full 30½-inch rough opening between rafters.

In **8-26** skylights were installed between heavy timber rafters. This enables very large skylights to be used, providing considerable natural light. In **8-27** skylights were installed along each side of the ridgeboard. Careful analysis of the structural requirements for the size of the ridgeboard and the supporting rafters is necessary when an application such as this is being planned. In **8-28** the rafters were kept 16 inches on center, providing considerable natural lighting. Before a roof window application such as this is used, the orientation of the window must receive careful consideration. Such an installation, when improperly oriented, could provide many hours of direct sunlight into the room, producing considerable heat and glare. Review Chapter 2 for information on locating windows and Chapter 5 for information on energy-efficient glazing.

Flashing the roof window properly is extremely important. The manufacturer will have flashing designed to fit the window and seal it watertight at the roofline. Most companies can provide flashing to accommodate any type of finished roofing (**8-29**). Typical flashing details are in **8-30**. The flashing is the same color as the aluminum used to clad the window.

8-26 These skylights or roof windows were installed between large timber rafters. This provides natural light and ventilation, and the timber rafters give the wall a unique depth.

8-27 These skylights were installed at the ridge, providing natural light for a long, windowless corridor.

WINDOWS & SKYLIGHTS

Courtesy Velux-America, Inc.

8-28 (Left) This large installation provides considerable natural light and, if the building is oriented to reduce solar exposure and energy-efficient glazing is used, the heat loss and gain will be reduced.

Courtesy Velux-America, Inc.

8-29 This roof window has flashing made by the manufacturer especially for this type of unit.

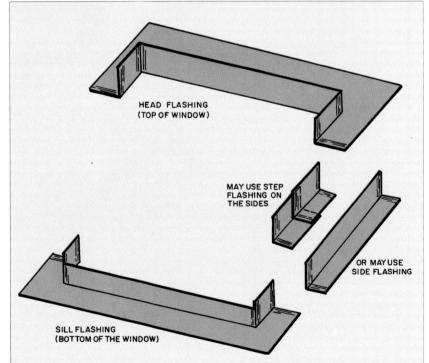

HEAD FLASHING
(TOP OF WINDOW)

MAY USE STEP
FLASHING ON
THE SIDES

OR MAY USE
SIDE FLASHING

SILL FLASHING
(BOTTOM OF THE WINDOW)

8-30 Flashing pieces such as these are generalized examples of manufacturer-supplied flashing.

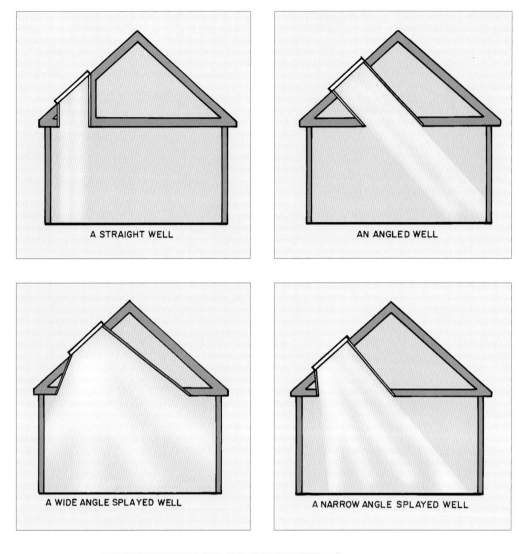

A STRAIGHT WELL

AN ANGLED WELL

A WIDE ANGLE SPLAYED WELL

A NARROW ANGLE SPLAYED WELL

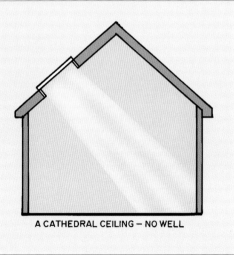

A CATHEDRAL CEILING – NO WELL

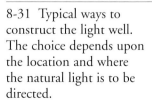

8-31 Typical ways to construct the light well. The choice depends upon the location and where the natural light is to be directed.

FRAMING
THE LIGHT WELL

If the skylight is in the roof of a room with a cathedral ceiling, the opening between the rafters projects the light into the room. This does not require additional framing. If the room has a ceiling, a light well must be constructed to carry the light through the attic. This is discussed in Chapter 2. The sides of a light well can be built perpendicular to the ceiling or on an angle or splayed as shown in **8-31**. The design used depends upon where the light is to be projected.

The actual framing is much like that for partition framing. It is important to securely join the studs to the roof and ceiling framing. They must be in alignment so when the drywall is installed it will not have bulges or recessed areas. The design of the framing will vary depending upon the experience and preferences of the carpenter. In **8-32** is framing for a straight light well and in **8-33** is framing for a flared light well.

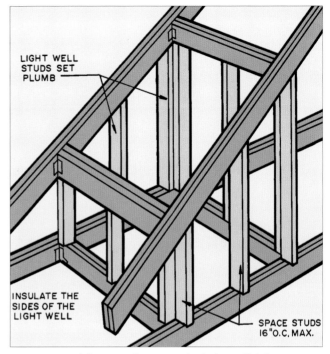

8-32 Typical framing for a straight light well. The main considerations are positioning the well for the desired light and aligning the studs properly so the finished drywall will be plumb and smooth.

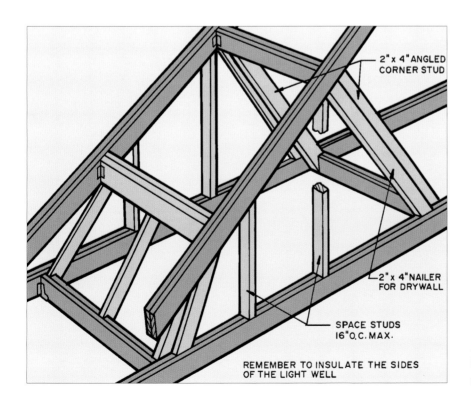

8-33 Typical framing for a flared light well.

8-34 A large, multi-sided dome skylight creates an attractive architectural feature.

8-35 The tower on a stone residence was roofed with a dome-type skylight.

8-36 Pyramid skylights are often used in a series. However, a single unit serves a residential room adequately.

8-37 A ridge skylight can be used to provide natural light to a large open area such as this indoor pool.

OTHER TYPES OF SKYLIGHT

Other types of skylight suitable for residential and commercial construction are available or should be considered as the house is planned. In **8-34** is a 12-sided dome skylight that creates a striking architectural feature. It was used to enclose a tower on a residence as shown in **8-35**. A pyramid skylight can provide considerable light and also adds a very interesting architectural detail (**8-36**).

A ridge skylight is suited to bringing natural light to a large open area, as shown in **8-37**.

INSTALLING TUBULAR SKYLIGHTS

The parts of a tubular skylight are seen in **8-38**. It comes as a complete unit ready to install. Installation instructions are included. Following is a generalized procedure.

Begin by locating the light tube on the ceiling. Locate it between the ceiling joists so no cutting or reinforcing is needed (**8-39**). Check in the attic to see whether there are any obstructions. The tube can be angled some, so it can miss any obstructions. However, watch for electric wires, plumbing, and any major structural members.

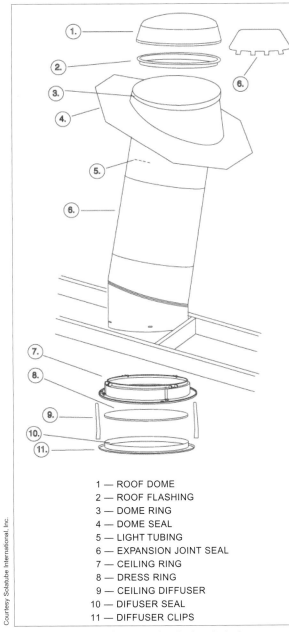

1 — ROOF DOME
2 — ROOF FLASHING
3 — DOME RING
4 — DOME SEAL
5 — LIGHT TUBING
6 — EXPANSION JOINT SEAL
7 — CEILING RING
8 — DRESS RING
9 — CEILING DIFFUSER
10 — DIFFUSER SEAL
11 — DIFFUSER CLIPS

8-38 The parts of a typical tubular skylight.

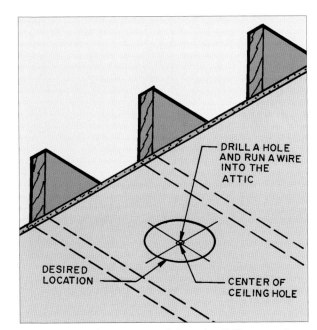

8-39 Locate the position of the tube diffuser on the ceiling. Keep it between the ceiling joists. Check in the attic for obstructions.

You could drill a hole in the center of the location and run a wire up into the attic to help you identify and position it. If there are obstructions, either move the location or plan to angle around them. The amount of offset between the ceiling mounting and the hole in the roof will depend upon the design of the tubular skylight (**8-40** and earlier in **8-19**).

If it is to be a straight tube, cut the hole in the ceiling. Drop a plumb line from the roof in the attic to the center of the ceiling hole (**8-41**). This locates the center of the roof hole. Cut the hole in the roof. If the pipe has an offset, measure over the distance from the center of the ceiling hole to locate the center of the offset roof hole (**8-42**).

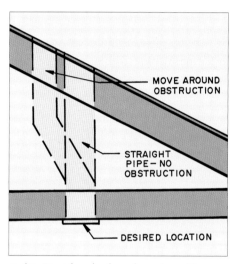

8-40 Decide whether the tube will run straight from the bubble on the roof or if it will have to be angled. Check the instructions to verify the amount of angle possible.

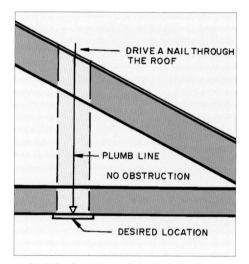

8-41 The location of the hole in the roof for a straight tube can be found by dropping a plumb line from the roof sheathing to the center of the hole in the ceiling.

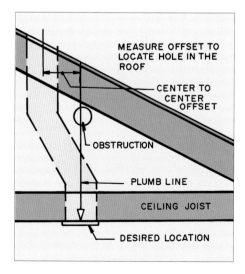

8-42 If an offset is required, measure over from the centerline of the hole in the ceiling a distance equal to the needed offset.

After the hole in the roof has been cut, install the flashing unit (**8-43**). Then assemble the other parts and seal them with the material supplied by the manufacturer (**8-44**). Finally, install the ceiling diffuser (**8-45**).

8-43 Install the flashing unit on the roof as directed by the manufacturer.

8-44 Install the components as instructed by the manufacturer. Here the flashing and bubble (dome) have been installed and the light tube is being slid up from the inside.

8-45 After the tube is in place, install the ceiling diffuser.

Sunrooms & Sunspaces

Adding some type of glass-enclosed space to a house provides a means of gaining a significant amount of solar heating in the winter. It also adds a very pleasant room to the house for relaxation, growing plants, and broad visual access to attractive exterior surroundings (9-1).

The terms used to describe these glazed spaces vary, including sunrooms, sunspaces, greenhouses, and patio rooms. The terms used in this chapter reflect the usage in construction dictionaries and the descriptions provided by the companies that manufacture various products.

Courtesy Four Seasons Solar Products Corporation

9-1 Sunrooms provide a pleasant living space and wide views of the surrounding countryside.

9-2 These movable insulated ceiling shades are used in the summer to block excessive solar energy and in the winter to help reduce heat loss through the glazing.

As you select and design a glazed living space for your house, it is important to chose one that has excellent watertight connections that allow the glass and frame to expand and contract with temperature changes yet do not leak. It is best if the room can be closed off from the house when extreme weather conditions make it difficult to heat or cool. Energy-efficient glazing is a must, and the best available should be used. See Chapters 4 and 5 for information on energy efficiency and glazing. If the space is to be mechanically heated and cooled, this should be planned as the room is selected. The size of the heating and cooling unit depends upon accurate information about the glazing and heat loss and gain through the aluminum framing. The walls and, in some cases, the roof should have moveable panels to allow excess heat to be vented and permit the inflow of cool, comfortable evening breezes. Consider installing movable ceiling shades. In **9-2** the ceiling shades have double air pockets and move on tracks with geared rollers. In the summer they block the sun in those hours when it hits the roof and in the winter help reduce heat loss.

If the heat generated in the glass room is to be used as a form of solar heating, it is necessary to provide some form of fan-and-duct system to move the heat into the house. If humidity is a problem and condensation forms on the inside of the glazing, have a means of reducing the humidity in the room. See more on condensation in Chapter 1.

GREENHOUSES

A greenhouse is a glass-enclosed structure primarily used for growing plants and vegetables under protected conditions. When it is properly designed and located, plants can be grown all year. What the plants need is natural light and the proper temperature for growth. This means using solar-heat gain in the winter and blocking and venting excess heat in the summer. In colder climates the greenhouse will require a heating system.

9-3 This aluminum-framed, glazed greenhouse is attached to the house, providing access from the house. The glazing is energy efficient as required for greenhouses.

9-4 The garden window provides a small growing area. Some have casement windows on the end to vent excess heat.

9-5 This aluminum-framed freestanding greenhouse uses a specially formulated glass called Wonderglas™. It is available in a wide range of sizes.

VARIETIES
OF GREENHOUSE

A greenhouse can be a simple addition to a house as shown in **9-3**, a small garden window unit (**9-4** and **9-5**), or a freestanding structure (**9-6**). Greenhouses are available as prefabricated kits with glazing to provide the growing conditions desired. They can also be site-built—there are companies making glazing and weather-tight connections for use on wood-framed greenhouses. A separate greenhouse properly landscaped provides an attractive feature on the property (**9-7**).

Courtesy Four Seasons Solar Products Corporation

9-6 A freestanding greenhouse is an attractive feature in a landscaped area.

9-7 Two examples of the value of providing adequate access to the sunroom. Wide access enhances the room to which it is connected as well as gives the sunroom graphic visibility. (Courtesy Four Seasons Solar Products Corporation)

9-8 This sunroom is framed using heavy extruded aluminum structural members.

SUNROOMS, PATIO ROOMS, SUNSPACES

The definitions of these terms vary and, in some cases, are used to describe the same type of structure. The term **sunspace** seems to be a general term used to describe a room designed to admit the sun's rays. For this discussion the term **sun-**

9-9 This wood-framed structural system may be pine or oak. The exterior surfaces exposed to the weather are clad with aluminum, providing a maintenance-free exterior.

room will be used to describe a glass-enclosed space (roof and walls) that is typically heated and air-conditioned. It is designed as an all-season living space. The term **patio room** will be used to describe a structure that is heated and air-conditioned, has walls of glass, and has a conventional roof.

GLAZING FOR SUNSPACES

Glass should be at a minimum double-glazed and, in some climates, triple-glazed. Low-E glazing, argon gas in the airspace between the glass panes, and possibly some tinting will often be used. Review Chapter 5 for more information on glazing. Four Seasons Solar Products Corporation has developed a special glass for sunrooms. The flat and curved glass panels have a coating composed of nine microscopic layers of chemicals that contribute to these being highly energy-efficient glazing products.

SUNROOMS

As just described, a sunroom has a glazed roof and walls. To provide year-long comfortable living conditions, it must be energy efficient. A sunroom is typically connected to the exterior wall of the house. The installation is enhanced when wide doors are placed in the wall, providing an open feeling and easy access, as seen earlier in **9-7**. It is helpful if provision can be made to close the opening when weather conditions become extreme. Sunrooms often have heating and cooling facilities that enhance year-round use. Many have sliding glass panels permitting them to be open in pleasant temperatures much like a screened porch.

The structural systems typically used include aluminum and wood. The aluminum framing is formed from specially designed aluminum extrusions (**9-8**). A wood-framed sunroom is shown in **9-9**. The exterior surfaces are aluminum-clad. The

9-10 This sunroom has a sloped roof connected to the exterior wall with a curved panel. From the inside it gives a very attractive full view of the surrounding area.

exposed surfaces are aluminum and glass glazing that provide a maintenance-free structure.

The design of sunrooms varies considerably. Study the choices available as you decide, and plan carefully how the sunroom will connect to the house. One design uses a curve between the roof and the exterior wall (**9-10**), while another has them meet at a horizontal member (**9-11**). Notice how this structural detail influences the interior appearance.

9-11 This sunroom has the roof and exterior wall meet at a horizontal structural member. This produces a different impression than the room in 9-10.

9-12 Sunrooms are available with gable and hipped roofs.

9-13 This unit has a peaked, multi-sided roof that provides a dramatic interior. It serves as a living and dining area.

9-14 A large dining area is located in this sunroom.

9-15 A sunroom can serve as an excellent location for a hot tub and exercise equipment.

Sunrooms with hipped and gable roof designs offer another distinctive appearance dependent on the structural details chosen, as shown in **9-12**.

In addition to the structural aspect of how the sunroom will connect with your house, the choice of a sunroom may also depend upon what activities are planned for the space. In **9-13** it is used as an area in which to relax and in **9-14** it provides a dining area. The sunroom in **9-15** is used as a fitness center including a hot tub. A large room can enclose a small swimming pool (**9-16**).

A very large solar structure sheltering a large pool is shown in **9-17**. It has an aluminum framework and triple-glazed polycarbonate panels. The roof admits natural light and contributes to passive solar heating of the vast interior.

9-16 A sunroom structure makes a nice enclosure for a small, private swimming pool.

9-17 This aluminum-framed, energy-efficient sunroom can span wide distances and serves well to enclose large swimming pools or areas for other activities.

9-18 This patio room has a standard roof system. The vinyl-framed wall-glazing panels are energy efficient.

PATIO ROOMS

As described earlier, a patio room has a conventional roof and glass walls. The roof provides considerable protection from the rays of the sun and when properly insulated is more energy efficient than the glazed walls. The rooms shown in the following illustrations have energy-efficient wall panels with vinyl frames providing a maintenance-free exterior. They open to natural ventilation. The room in **9-18** has a gable roof that, when used as a cathedral ceiling, provides an especially attractive interior. A typical flat-roof patio room is shown in **9-19**. This product uses a special snap-in aluminum roof panel that has a gutter along each edge of the roof.

Patio rooms are used for the same activities as discussed for sunrooms.

9-19 Patio rooms with a flat or slightly sloped roof have the interior ceiling like that in conventional construction.

Courtesy PGT Industries

Sun Shielding

As you plan your house, shielding of the windows should be considereed in the design to protect from the summer sun while allowing solar energy into the house in the winter. Traditional solutions to sun-screening have included the incorporation of a front or back porch (**10-1**). The earlier chapters of this book discuss energy-efficient glazing and the consideration of the orientation of the house in relation to the sun in the geographic area in which it is located. In addition there are other things that can be done to provide solar control.

10-1 Porches provide full sun screening but can make the rooms behind them a bit dark.

WINDOW OVERHANGS

Window overhangs block the sun from striking the glass and heating it. This is definitely more effective than interior sun-shading devices such as blinds or curtains. If the sun hits the glass, it gets hot and radiates heat into the room even though an interior shading device is in place.

Overhanging devices are especially important on the south side of the house because it has the longest exposure to the sun. The east wall gets the low early morning sun and the west wall the low late-afternoon sun. The actual shading will vary depending upon the geographic area. The example in **10-2** shows the theory behind this method of shading. In the summer the sun's rays approach on a steeper angle than in the winter. This permits the overhang to provide summer protection, and yet allows some sun to enter the windows in the winter, providing some solar heat.

A **roof overhang** as shown in **10-2** is probably the most frequently used shading method. The addition of a louvered sunshade (**10-3**) is just as effective but does affect the appearance of the

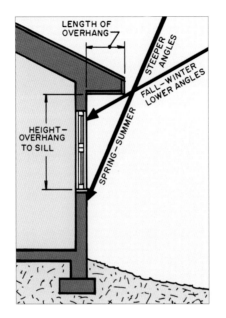

10-2 The angle of the sun's rays toward the earth in the northern hemisphere is steeper in the summer than in the winter.

house. It has the advantage that the louvers can be made adjustable so they can regulate the sun's rays according to the season.

An **awning** is another type of overhanging sun shield (**10-4**). It provides very effective screening. Most awnings made with fabric covers can be folded up against the house when they are not needed. Metal awnings are not retractable.

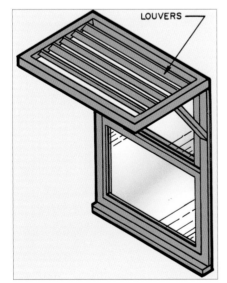

10-3 Louvered sunshades provide adjustable window sun screening.

10-4 Canvas and metal awnings provide excellent sun screens. It is best if they can be moved up out of the way after the sun has passed.

Metal awnings do block the sun's rays in the winter, reducing solar-heating possibilities. Some have ventilated openings releasing trapped heat. Both metal and fabric awnings are available in several colors. Remember, they do become a prominent part of the exterior appearance of the house.

Porches also can serve as solar screening devices. They tend to make the room dark, because some of the natural light is blocked, and they definitely change the exterior appearance of the house, as een earlier in **10-1**. A **balcony** can also make a satisfactory screen (**10-5**).

10-5 A balcony is an interesting architectural feature and serves as an excellent sun screen.

ROOF OVERHANG

The size of the roof overhang will vary depending upon the parallel of latitude, appearance of the house, and the expected amount of shielding the windows need to provide from the hot summer sun. The angle of the sun's rays is different at each degree of latitude and at any given time of the day. The United States falls within parallels of latitude from 50 degrees to 25 degrees (**10-6**). The length and effects of the climate on heating and cooling vary depending upon the location. In northern states the heating season is longer and the cooling season shorter than in the central and southern states. In the southern states the cooling season is long and the heating season short.

OVERHANGS FOR CLIMATES IN THE NORTHERN HEMISPHERE

The following examples show how geographic location will affect the screening by a roof overhang. The penetration and screening of the sun in the examples are based on the window and wall construction shown in **10-7**. These are general-

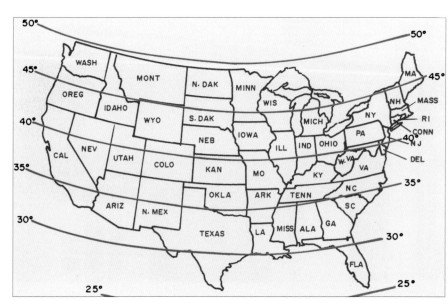

10-6 The continental United States falls within several parallels of latitude.

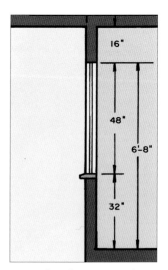

10-7 Overhang examples are based on this size window and sill height.

ized examples of the sun's rays in each parallel of latitude. Exact angles could be determined for a specific latitude, as desired. Obviously a longer window or sliding glass door will admit more sunlight. In the southern regions large overhangs are common. In the northern regions smaller overhangs are typical. For a specific house in a specific location, make a scale drawing like those shown to get a more accurate picture of the exposure that will occur. Most roof overhangs will provide some protection from the sun's rays but seldom give total protection because they would then have to be very wide. A combination of a nice overhang plus other screening devices, such as shades, blinds, and energy-efficient glazing, provides a total solution.

50-DEGREE PARALLEL

Examples for sun exposure in the 50-degree parallel of latitude are shown in **10-8**. The heating season typically runs from September through April. It is important that the overhang permit admission of as much solar heat as possible. The cooling season is short and not a major factor.

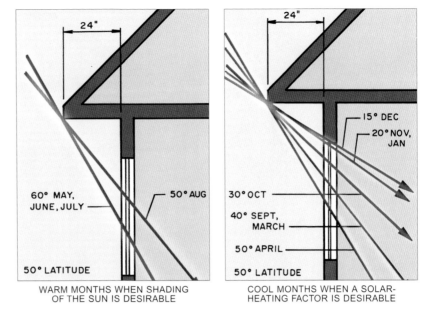

WARM MONTHS WHEN SHADING OF THE SUN IS DESIRABLE

COOL MONTHS WHEN A SOLAR-HEATING FACTOR IS DESIRABLE

10-8 Typical angles of the sun's rays in the northern United States around the 50-degree parallel of latitude for a 24-inch overhang.

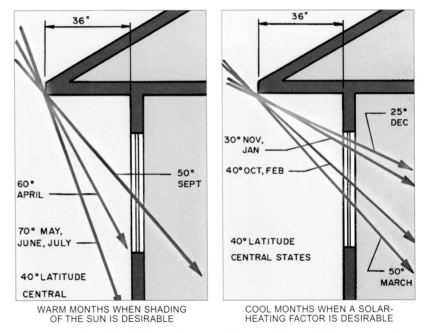

WARM MONTHS WHEN SHADING OF THE SUN IS DESIRABLE

COOL MONTHS WHEN A SOLAR-HEATING FACTOR IS DESIRABLE

10-9 Typical angles of the sun's rays in the central United States around the 40-degree parallel of latitude for a 36-inch overhang.

40-DEGREE PARALLEL

For the central United States around the 40-degree parallel of latitude, seasons during which heating and cooling are desirable are about the same length. For six months protection from solar penetration is desiraable, and for six months the admission of solar energy is helpful (**10-9**).

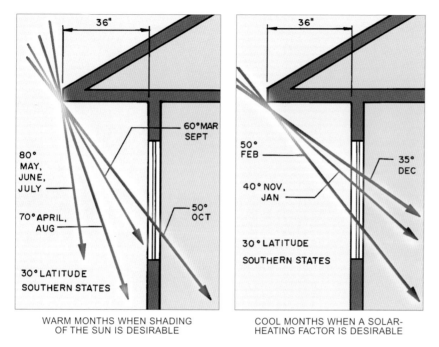

WARM MONTHS WHEN SHADING
OF THE SUN IS DESIRABLE

COOL MONTHS WHEN A SOLAR-
HEATING FACTOR IS DESIRABLE

10-10 Typical angles of the sun's rays in the southern United States around the 40-degree parallel of latitude for a 36-inch overhang.

30-DEGREE PARALLEL

The examples in **10-10** show that around the 30-degree parallel of latitude the season when cooling is desirable can run as long as eight months. Protection from the sun's penetration is a major consideration. This area will have large roof overhangs, yet the angle of the sun's rays is such that some solar heat can be available during the few cooler months. The 36-inch overhang provides considerable protection in the summer.

OTHER EXTERIOR SCREENING TECHNIQUES

The use of **bamboo, reed,** or **plastic reed roll-up shades** on the exterior of a window will reduce the influx of solar heat somewhat. They have the advantage of allowing some natural light to enter the room (**10-11**).

Louvered insect screens can be installed on each window and door glazing (**10-12**). The slates are on a fixed angle, so they will be more effective at certain times of the year than at other times. Low-angle rays will pass between the louvers, so more early-morning sun from the east and late-afternoon sun from the west will pass through windows facing east

10-11 Bamboo and reed roll-up shades are most effective when placed on the outside of the window.

and west than through those on the south side of the house. In the winter the screens can be removed.

Shutters can be installed on the inside of each window (**10-13**). Generally louvered shutters are used. Even when closed they admit some natural light. In very hot tropical climates shutters are often installed on the exterior of the window. If insulated shutters are used, they will provide some protection against heat loss in the winter.

Some protection can be had by erecting a **fence** (**10-14**). This provides some shade part of the day and a degree of privacy. It also blocks any view of the exterior yard or of an attractive scene in the distance. A fence will not provide much screening during the middle of the day but will work better on the east and west sides because the sun's rays are lower. The fence should be louvered or have staggered spaced boards on each side to allow some natural ventilation to the house. The view of these tall fences can be softened by planting shrubs in front of them. A trellis covered with vines is another nice way to provide some sun-screening. The area between the fence and the house reflects less heat on the

LOUVERED INSECT SCREEN

10-12 Louvered insect screens effectively divert the rays of the sun much of the time.

OPEN — NATURAL LIGHT IS ADMITTED AND THERE IS AN OUTSIDE VIEW

CLOSED — THERE IS PRIVACY AND PROTECTION FROM THE SUN'S RAYS

10-13 Louvered shutters protect from the sun and are decorative.

HORIZONTAL OR VERTICAL LOUVERS

STAGGER VERTICAL BOARDS

FENCE

TRELLIS

GRASS BETTER THAN SAND OR ROCK

wall when it is covered with grass rather than stone or sand or is paved with concrete. Overall a fence must be quite close to the house to shade the wall during the hot summer months.

A fence may block the sun's rays in the winter when solar energy is wanted to heat the house. Keep this in mind if a fence is planned. Refer to the examples shown earlier in **10-8** through **10-10** for typical solar angles in various geographic areas.

10-14 Various types of fence can provide screening from a low-angle sun.

10-15 Tall shrubs provide good screening and permit the air to filter through, making natural ventilation available.

10-16 Pleated shades block the admission of the sun's rays yet permit some light to show through.

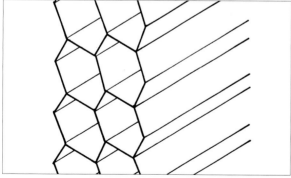

10-17 Fabric shades having two or three honeycomb air cells block the sun's rays and considerable heat transfer. The shades shown are on the ceiling of an all-glass sunroom.

A row of **tall shrubs** or **trees** with dense foliage provides good sun screening. They are very effective on the east and west walls. Consider planting deciduous trees, because they lose their leaves in the winter, permitting the sun's rays to strike the windows (**10-15**).

INTERIOR SUN-SCREENING TECHNIQUES

Remember that the interior shading techniques allow solar heat to penetrate to the interior of the house. These techniques allow for the absorption and radiation of the heat to the interior. The most effective types have reflective qualities and are made of a material that absorbs little solar energy.

The most commonly used interior sun-screening device is some form of shade. **Pleated shades** are widely used (**10-16**). They are available as a single layer of fabric or with single or double air pockets (**10-17**).

Another efficient shade is made with a special solar-screen fabric from high-strength polyester or fiberglass yarn with a vinyl-compound coating (**10-18**). It is made in various densities. It does not radiate heat, it reduces heat infiltration, and it allows some visibility and natural light. A motor-controlled operating system is available.

Venetian blinds have the advantage of allowing you to adjust the angle of the slats to block the sun's rays at any time of the day and admit considerable natural light most of the time (**10-19**). As mentioned in Chapter 5, narrow venetian-blind slats are installed in the airspace between some double-glazed windows. These provide good solar control yet can be opened when wanted to admit natural light.

Draperies can also block entrance of the sun's rays. They typically move along a track at the top of the window and so are easy to open and close (**10-20**). Insulated draperies consisting of several layers of fabric and a liner are available. They are also useful in the winter to reduce heat loss from the windows.

The use of exterior and interior shading devices is not as essential when energy-efficient glazing is used. Double and triple glazing with argon or krypton gas in the airspace, the use of low-E coating, and tint screens reduce the need for these devices. However, those with older houses having less efficient windows will find these devices very rewarding.

Courtesy VIMCO

10-18 This shading system uses a special solar-screen fabric. It reduces heat transfer and ultraviolet rays.

10-19 Venetian blinds can be adjusted to block the admission of the sun and opened to admit natural light when the sun has passed. They do absorb heat, however, and radiate it to the air in the room.

10-20 Draperies are effective sun blockers. Insulated draperies also reduce heat loss in the winter.

10-21 A large expanse of glass can admit a great amount of solar energy, creating excessive interior heat and exposing the occupants to damaging ultraviolet rays. Solar-control window film has been applied, reducing these unfavorable circumstances as well as glare.

SOLAR-CONTROL WINDOW FILMS

Solar-control window film is applied to clear glazing that is already installed. Trained technicians install it. It is an invisible film made with a laminate of polyester and metallic coatings combined with a clear, distortion-free adhesive system and a scratch-resistant face coating providing almost total optical clarity. The film can be applied to single- and double-pane window glass (**10-21**). More information on window films is in Chapter 5.

There are various types of solar-control window film available. Some are especially effective in reducing the passage of damaging ultraviolet rays and reduce sun glare (**10-22**). As a film is selected, the needs for the installation must be decided. Is the reduction in ultraviolet transmission a major feature, or the reduction of glare

BEFORE COVERING WITH A SOLAR-CONTROL FILM

AFTER THE SOLAR-CONTROL FILM WAS APPLIED

10-22 Solar-control window film reduces glare and ultraviolet penetration.

or heat transfer? For example, if a film that primarily reduces glare is chosen, it will have a low light-transmission factor. If the windows face south and the house is in a warm climate, solar-heat rejection will probably be more important. The final choice will be a balance between visible-light transmission, resistance to ultraviolet transmission, solar-energy reduction, shading, and glare reduction. Manufacturers have extensive data on these factors for their range of film products.

Index

For additional information see the *Installer Training Manual* and *Installation Video,* available from the American Architectural Manufacturers Association, 1827 Walden Office Square, Suite 104, Schaumburg, IL 60173-4268, and *Window and Door Installation, A440.4-98,* available from the Canadian Standards Association, 178 Rexdale Blvd., Etobicoke, ON M9W IRS Canada

Metric Equivalents

[to the nearest mm, 0.1cm, or 0.01m]

inches	mm	cm	inches	mm	cm	inches	mm	cm
⅛	3	0.3	13	330	33.0	38	965	96.5
¼	6	0.6	14	356	35.6	39	991	99.1
⅜	10	1.0	15	381	38.1	40	1016	101.6
½	13	1.3	16	406	40.6	41	1041	104.1
⅝	16	1.6	17	432	43.2	42	1067	106.7
¾	19	1.9	18	457	45.7	43	1092	109.2
⅞	22	2.2	19	483	48.3	44	1118	111.8
1	25	2.5	20	508	50.8	45	1143	114.3
1¼	32	3.2	21	533	53.3	46	1168	116.8
1½	38	3.8	22	559	55.9	47	1194	119.4
1¾	44	4.4	23	584	58.4	48	1219	121.9
2	51	5.1	24	610	61.0	49	1245	124.5
2½	64	6.4	25	635	63.5	50	1270	127.0
3	76	7.6	26	660	66.0			
3½	89	8.9	27	686	68.6	inches	feet	m
4	102	10.2	28	711	71.1			
4½	114	11.4	29	737	73.7	12	1	0.31
5	127	12.7	30	762	76.2	24	2	0.61
6	152	15.2	31	787	78.7	36	3	0.91
7	178	17.8	32	813	81.3	48	4	1.22
8	203	20.3	33	838	83.8	60	5	1.52
9	229	22.9	34	864	86.4	72	6	1.83
10	254	25.4	35	889	88.9	84	7	2.13
11	279	27.9	36	914	91.4	96	8	2.44
12	305	30.5	37	940	94.0	108	9	2.74

Conversion Factors

1 mm	=	0.039 inch	1 inch	=	25.4 mm	mm	=	millimeter
1 m	=	3.28 feet	1 foot	=	304.8 mm	cm	=	centimeter
1 m²	=	10.8 square feet	1 square foot	=	0.09 m²	m	=	meter
						m²	=	square meter